Mentally Ill
Inmates
and Corrections

An Explorative, Insightful, and Pragmatic Approach

Elvis Slaughter, MSCJ
Retired-Superintendent of Corrections

World Press Publishing
Elvis Slaughter
P. O. Box 314
Calumet City, IL 60409
Eslaugh108@aol.com

Library of Congress Control Number: 2021903796

www.worldpresspublishing.com

Printed in the United States of America

Contents

Introduction

Mentally Ill Inmates and Corrections is an explorative, insightful, and pragmatic approach to help criminal justice professionals, students, and career correctional settings employees understand inmates with mental illnesses. Research incorporated into this text draws from the last several decades, in order to best identify patterns, trends, and changes that have occurred within the correctional system.

Most infamous criminals in the United States have actually been identified as having suffered from some form of mental illness. It is important to note that the number of criminals with mental illness represents just a small fraction of individuals diagnosed with mental illness, and most of those suffering from a mental illness do not engage in criminal activity when properly treated and given adequate social support. Forensic psychologists often examine the mental correlates of criminality in the wake of a robbery, violent assault, or murder. The results have indicated that many criminals have been diagnosed with mental illness and some may be suffering from co-occurring substance abuse.

Among the most common psychological disorders suffered by some of history's most infamous criminals in the US is schizophrenia. One such criminal identified as schizophrenic was David Berkowitz, commonly known as "Son of Sam." In the 1970s, he killed six persons and claimed that he was told to do it by his neighbor's dog. He was also diagnosed with paranoid schizophrenia. James Eagan Holmes was previously standing trial for the 2012 "Batman murders" that took place in Aurora, Colorado. He was diagnosed with schizophrenia by 20 different doctors. Richard Chase, another criminal identified as schizophrenic, killed six people in California. He was known as the "vampire of Sacramento" due to the fact that he went on to the drink the blood of his victims.

Another mental disorder that is common among criminals is borderline personality disorder. Some notorious killers diagnosed with this mental disorder include Aileen Wuornos, who confessed to seven murders in Florida, Jeffrey Dahmer, also known as the "Milwaukee Cannibal" after he killed seventeen boys and men between 1978 and 1991, and Kristen H. Gilbert, a nurse who killed four patients by administering fatal doses of epinephrine to induce cardiac arrest while working at a Northampton Virginia hospital.

The third type of mental disorder most commonly associated is antisocial personality disorder, which was the diagnosis for the three most ruthless serial killers in the US. This included Ted Bundy, who confessed to killing 30 people in the 1970s, and Charles Manson, leader of the "Manson Family" cult and the mastermind behind the 1969 murders at the home of Sharon Tate. The third was John Wayne Gacy, also known as "Killer Clown", who raped and killed 33 boys and young men in the 1970s (Forensics College).

One of the mental disorders that many mental ill inmates and serial killers have in common is anti-social personality disorder (ADP). Unfortunately, it does not often have a clinical diagnosis. However, some mentally ill inmates and serial killers also suffer from some deeper mental illness, such as bipolar disorder, schizophrenia or borderline personality disorder. These are some of the mental disorders that affect an individual's ability to determine what is right or wrong (Ranker Crime).

For the corrections systems that are not equipped or designed to provide mental health services, the high prevalence of individuals with mental illnesses has capacity, budgetary, as well as staffing ramifications; a high number of individuals having mental illnesses affect the provision of constitutionally mandated treatment not only for "inside the walls," but also for community transition planning and reentry services and community corrections caseloads.

Some questions that easily come to mind at this point include: are the mentally ill more likely to commit crimes? Are individuals who engage in criminal activities more predisposed to mental illness? Is the correctional facility the right place for a person with a mental illness? These questions are not easy to answer, but this book will attempt to answer as much as possible.

The policy-driven transfer of the seriously mentally ill persons from mental health care facilities to secure punishment facilities is so pervasive that it has earned its own descriptive term "trans-institution-alization." Healthcare of any kind in most American jails, as well as prisons, is substandard and when mental health care is available, it's often limited to few a very overworked mental health professionals that may not be able to focus beyond whether an inmate (or a patient) is likely going to commit suicide in the near future (Zoukis, 2018).

This text will seek to explore the issues that the mentally ill inmates face in most correctional facilities, the problems with solitary confinement and how it affects mentally ill inmates, the role of correctional officers as well as healthcare professionals, and possible solutions that will help in dealing with the rising caseload of mental illnesses in correctional institutions.

CHAPTER 1:
A History of Mental Illness & Prisons

"On any given day, at least 284,000 schizophrenic and manic-depressive individuals are incarcerated, and 547, 800 are on probation... These statistics represent countless backwards steps that have been made in the name of progress. They remind me of what the governor of Virginia said when he expressed dismay that he was 'forced to authorize the confinement of persons with mental illnesses in the Williamsburg jail, against both his conscience and the law,' because of lack of appropriate services. That was in 1773."

- Congressman Ted Strickland (Crime Times, 2003)

Currently, there is a staggering number of mentally ill persons confined in various jails and prisons across the United States. In fact, it is estimated by experts that the figures range between two and four hundred thousand mentally ill inmates. There are various factors behind the massive number of incarcerated mentally ill persons, however, mental health professionals, as well as correction professionals, unanimously point to the fact that the primary cause of such an increase is the inadequate provision of mental health services as well as the country's punitive criminal justice policies (Drapkin, 2003).

Most mentally ill persons who end up in jail are initially incarcerated in jails as pretrial detainees and it is interesting to note that two of the largest mental health providers in the United States are Los

Angeles County and Cook County jails (Sacramento Bee, March 17, 1999).

Colonial Era

Jails, as well as prisons, have always been home to mentally ill persons in colonial America. In modern America, a non-violent, unstable person is often allowed to remain at home while those who are violent or assaultive are confined in prisons across the United States. In fact, legislation was passed as early as 1694 in the Massachusetts Bay Colony which granted the authority to confine an individual who is considered a dangerous threat to the peace and safety of others, in order to prevent such dangerous people from going out of control.

In those days, the jailers were often provided with a fee which was paid by the mentally ill person's family or by the town that is confining him. It was once recorded that the churchwardens paid the town marshal in New York City two shillings and six pence weekly to help keep Robert Bullman, a declared 'madman', in prison. Despite the widespread practice, voices of protest in colonies started to emerge, claiming that it was inhumane to confine persons that were mentally ill to jails (Deutsch, 1937).

The impact of these sentiments contributed to the creation and admission of the first patients into the first psychiatric ward in Pennsylvania Hospital in Philadelphia in 1752. Later in 1773, permission was given by the Virginia Governor Francis Fauquier to build the first hospital in Williamsburg, exclusively for those considered insane. The governor later acknowledged that he felt compelled to authorize the confinement of insane persons in Williamsburg prison, both against the law and his conscience, claiming he had no alternative (Ibid).

Post-Colonial Era

After the creation of the United States, there were many claims by citizens that keeping mentally ill persons in prisons was uncivilized and inhumane, and these claims increased into the 1820s with the establishment of organizations such as the Boston Prison Discipline Society, founded by Reverend Louis Dwight in 1825. His insistence that lunatic persons were supposed to be kept in hospitals struck a responsive chord amongst people, especially when his investigation revealed that a significant number of mentally ill persons were actually confined in circumstances that were degrading, both emotionally and physically.

Consequently, a committee was appointed by the Massachusetts state legislature in 1827 to investigate the conditions of state prisons. In the report of the committee, shocking revelations of the conditions of the lunatic persons that were confined were made; in clear terms, they stated that *"Less attention is paid to their cleanliness and comfort than to the wild beasts in their cages, which are kept for show"* (Grob, 1966).

As a result, the committee recommended that confining the mentally ill in jails and prisons would be declared illegal. This led to the approval of the state psychiatric hospital in Worcester, capable of housing 120 patients. It was recorded that when the hospital opened in 1833, more than half of all the people admitted in the first year were actually transferred from prisons, jails, and almshouses (Deutsch, 1937).

Continual efforts were made to stop the imprisonment of mentally ill persons, including a campaign by Dorothea Dix, who visited 18 state prisons as well as 300 county jails. This type of campaigning led to a gradual acceptance of the fact that mentally ill persons are supposed to be kept in mental hospitals. By 1875, a significant number of mentally ill persons, who were originally confined to jails and prisons, were transferred to about 75 different public psychiatric hospitals in various states throughout the U.S. (Wines, 1888).

From the 1870s to the 1970s, it was generally assumed throughout the US that individuals deemed mentally ill were no longer supposed to be in jail or prisons but in hospitals specifically for mentally ill people, along with the expectation that they would be properly treated there. During this time, it was recorded that there was a low rate of mentally ill persons in jails and prisons (Bromberg, 1937). So, for about 100 years, the issue of mentally ill persons in jails and prisons appeared resolved since these mentally ill persons were treated as patients rather than as criminals (Torrey, 2002).

The Effects of Deinstitutionalization

In the 1960s deinstitutionalization is a government policy that led to the movement of mentally ill persons out of "insane asylums" that were run by the state, and into community mental health centers that were federally funded. This move focused on improving the treatment of the mentally ill and aimed to cut the government budget, however, it led to several issues (Amadeo, 2018).

States started downsizing and closing their public mental health hospitals in the 1960s. As the state mental hospitals began to release most of their patients during this time, there came a gradual change to the prevailing practice of keeping the mentally ill persons in mental health hospitals. This medical-social policy was actually implemented with good intentions but was poorly planned because it lacked proper follow-up psychiatric care of most of the patients that were discharged from the mental hospitals (Council of State Governments, New York, 2002).

There were several factors that precipitated this process:

1. Federal funding from programs such as Medicare and Medicaid were no longer channeled toward mental hospitals and were instead channeled toward mental health centers (Amadeo, 2018).
2. The first generation of effective antipsychotic medications were developed, which ensured the continued treatment of mentally ill persons outside the hospital. Some of these medications include clozapine and chlorpromazine.
3. Also, litigation led to an increase in the due process safeguards in mental hospitals regarding the process for involuntary commitment, as well as release procedures. This meant that the number of people that were kept in the mental hospitals against

their will was greatly reduced (Council of State Governments, New York, 2002).

Consequently, many of the patients relapsed into psychosis, while a number of them even went on to commit several felonies or misdemeanor acts, acts often associated with untreated mental illnesses. Some were arrested for such crimes without the state of their mental health being taken into consideration. The consequences and effects of deinstitutionalization on the population of inmates in correctional facilities was becoming more apparent by the early 1970s. The rapid increase in the number of imprisoned, mentally ill persons in the San Mateo County jail was actually described by Marc Abramson, a psychiatrist, as the *"criminalization of mentally ill disordered behavior."* Prisons began to drown in patients and this increase was observed by many states in the mid-1970s (Abramson, 1972).

This led to several studies of psychiatric care, which were carried out in both federal and state prisons in 1978 and 1980. One study, published in 1980, was on "500 defendants that were in need of psychiatric treatment" and came to the conclusion that emptying the hospitals had led to an increase in the number of deinstitutionalized patients forced into the criminal justice system. By the early 1980s, it was very clear that deinstitutionalization was contributing to a progressive increase in the number of persons who were mentally ill within the criminal justice system, and thus, the discharge of persons having serious mental illness without any process to ensure they had been given proper treatment for their condition was definitely a prescription for disaster (Hornbeck, 1997).

The situation continued to worsen into the early 1980s, as some officials estimated that around 10 percent of inmates in prisons and jails had serious mental illnesses. There were doubts regarding where these mentally ill inmates came from, but a study of 132 patients discharged in 1988 from Ohio state hospital revealed that 17 percent of those that were released were arrested within a period of six months (Belcher, 1988). This condition did not get better in the 1990s, but rather, continued to deteriorate, as a 1992 survey revealed. This survey of 1,371 jails across the United States reported how various minor offenses, often linked with untreated mental illness, led to the incarceration of individuals (Torrey et al., 1992).

In 1998, a survey by the Federal Department of Justice noted that "16 percent of State prison inmates… [as well as]16 percent of persons in local jails either reported an overnight stay in a mental hospital or having a mental condition" (Ditton, 1999). The situation is no longer eliciting as much public or professional reaction, despite the steady and continuous increase in the number of persons who are mentally ill in most correctional facilities (Hermes, 2007). In 2010, the Treatment Advocacy Center reported that in the US as a whole, the number of seriously mentally ill persons in prisons and jails is now more than three times the number in hospitals. The states with the worst number of mentally ill inmates are Nevada and Arizona, with each state having around ten times more than other states (Torrey et al., 2010).

The Aftermath of Deinstitutionalization

In 2006, the Department of Justice reported that 24 percent of prisoners in local jails and 15 percent of inmates in state prisons were deemed psychotic.

While deinstitutionalization continued into the next decade, the condition of some of the correctional facilities in the United States also became increasingly deplorable: (James et al., 2006)

➤ The closure of the Georgia Mental Health Institute led to an increase of 73.74 percent of the number of inmates in the county jail that were being treated for mental illness.

➤ The head of the local county jail in Northwest Georgia reported that there was an increase of 60 percent in the number of inmate's mental health problems after the Northwest Georgia Regional Hospital was closed (Simmons, 2006).

➤ Ohio's Stark County Jail reported an increase of 30 percent in the number of inmates with serious mental illnesses.

➤ Missouri's Boone County Jail reported a 30 percent increase in the number of inmates with mental illnesses.

- ➤ Texas' El Paso County Jail reported a 40 percent increase in the number of inmates with serious mental illnesses.
- ➤ Pennsylvania's Erie County Jail reported a 44 percent increase, while Iowa's Black Hawk County Jail reported a 60 percent increase in the number of inmates with serious mental illnesses (Hermes, 2007).

Merits and Demerits of Deinstitutionalization

Although deinstitutionalization caused a number of issues for correctional institutions, it still provided several benefits:

- ➤ Deinstitutionalization offered more rights to mentally ill persons since a majority of mentally ill individuals kept in mental hospitals lived in backwaters for decades.
- ➤ The culture of treatment of mentally ill persons changed from "send them away" and made the reintegration of such persons into society possible.
- ➤ Individuals with Down syndrome, as well as other high-functioning mental disorders, benefited from the policy (Amadeo, 2018).

Demerits

Obviously, the disadvantages of the process far outweigh the advantages. Some of the issues caused by the deinstitutionalization policy include:

- ➤ A majority of the severely mentally ill individuals were among those that were released from the institutions. This group of people were not actually the right candidates for community centers because of the nature of their illnesses. They required long-term, in-patient care which would provide them better treatment.
- ➤ Since the federal funding for the mental health centers was insufficient, there were also insufficient centers available to

meet the mental health needs of mentally ill persons. The inadequate funding also made it difficult to create comprehensive programs for treatment and rehabilitation.

➢ Since the community resources were scattered throughout a city, mental health professionals greatly underestimated the difficulties associated with coordinating these resources for people with disorders, making accessibility challenging, sometimes even impossible.

➢ The courts also made it extremely hard to commit people against their will whether it was for the welfare and safety of the individual himself or others (Amadeo, 2018).

Presently, the number of people being treated for various mental illnesses in state hospitals has greatly reduced within the last few decades, while the federal, state, and county prisons have recorded an increase in the number of offenders with mental illness and they often lack the ability to provide proper care and treatment (Lee, 2015).

CHAPTER 2:
An Overview of Mental Illness in Correctional Facilities

"We've, frankly, criminalized the mentally ill, and used local jails as de facto mental health institutions,"

-Alex Briscoe
(Health director for Alameda County
Jail in northern California) (Varney, 2014)

The level of serious mental illness in inmates in various correctional facilities in the United States has become so prevalent that prisons and jails are now referred to as "the new asylums." It is interesting to note that correctional facilities like Chicago's Cook County Jail, Los Angeles County Jail, and New York's Riker's Island have more mentally ill persons than the remaining psychiatric hospitals in the US (Torrey et al., 2014). Mentally ill inmates are often incarcerated for a longer period of time than other inmates because it is not easy for them to adhere to prison and jail rules. According to one study, mentally ill inmates in Washington state prisons accounted for about 41 percent of all infractions despite the fact that they constituted just 19 percent of the population in prison (Torrey et al., 2010).

There are approximately 7,500 inmates housed on any given day at the Cook County Jail. The Cook County Jail is notorious for being known as a so-called dumping ground for the mentally ill. In a 2015 report, The Atlantic revealed that 1 in 3 inmates suffered from some form of mental illness. In the first 10 months of 2017, 222 detainees in the Cook County Jail were <u>charged</u> with indecent exposure, including masturbation towards female staff. In more than half of those cases of exposure, the victims worked at the jail. The numerous other victims included court lawyers and court staff (Peck, 2017). Many of these inmates have labeled themselves as Salvages.

The level of mental health and behavioral problems among prisoners has been gradually becoming more severe. Sometimes, psychiatric patients being treated for their disorder find themselves entangled within the criminal justice system. For example, in 2012, it was reported by researchers that 12 percent of adult psychiatric patients being treated in the San Diego County health system were incarcerated. Similarly, in Connecticut in 2013, 28 percent of residents that were currently being treated for bipolar disorder or schizophrenia had either been arrested or detained.

Some of the individuals with mental illnesses, both in our communities as well as in prisons, suffer from several mental disorders that are serious enough to require proper psychiatric treatment. However, the symptoms of some of these conditions are subtle and can only be discerned and diagnosed by trained clinicians, especially for inmates who are suffering from serious cases of depression, which may manifest through unsociable and withdrawn behaviors to correctional staff and other inmates (Torrey et al., 2010).

Additionally, symptoms of other serious mental illnesses of inmates can be identified easily with the layman's eye, especially with some of the more specific behaviors that inmates exhibit, such as:

➢ Mumbling incoherently
➢ Staring fixedly at the prison walls
➢ Biting chunks of their flesh from their bodies
➢ Rubbing feces on their bodies
➢ Hallucinating
➢ Slashing themselves
➢ Ranting and raving
➢ Sticking pencils in their penises

Along with the general problem of the increasing numbers of mentally ill inmates, individuals whose mental illnesses can be specifically classified as severe are being incarcerated in increasing numbers as well. In the words of the lead psychologist at Washington State's McNeil Island Correctional Center, *"the severity of the mental illness of those coming in is increasing. People are no longer going to state hospitals. The prisoners often have no idea how they ended up here"* (Human Rights Watch, 2003).

About 73 percent of women in state prisons, as well as 55 percent of men, have a minimum of one mental health condition. Additionally, 61 percent of women and 44 percent of men in federal prisons experience at least one mental health problem during their incarceration period. It has also been noted that 62 percent of men and 75 percent of women in local jails also suffer from at least one mental health problem. It is estimated that those incarcerated with serious mental illness in the US are now three times more than those in mental hospitals.

Oftentimes, inmates struggling with some form of a mental health condition, are people who have witnessed or experienced traumatic events during their adolescence. The correctional facility is not the best place for mentally ill persons. Suffering from the mental health problem is stressful already, but when one is placed into the jail environment, it becomes even more stressful. Many of these inmates are kept in seclusion for an extended period of time, which further worsens their condition. It was revealed by the Department of Justice that 20 percent of prisoners having some form of mental illness were wounded in jailhouse fights, in comparison to 10 percent of prisoners without any mental illness (PBS, 2014).

When evaluating the financial impacts, it is more expensive to keep mentally ill inmates in jail as opposed to other inmates for several reasons, including the need for more staff. For instance, according to the reports of one study, the average cost of maintaining an average inmate in Texas prisons is about $22,000 each year, however, the cost range for inmates with mental illness is from $30,000 to $50,000 each year. A significant portion of the increase of the financial burden is linked to psychiatric medications, as well as the cost of losing or settling lawsuits as a result of the treatment of inmates that are mentally ill (Miller & Fantz, 2007, Bender, 2003 and Gottschlich & Cetnar 2002).

Facts about the Prevalence of Mental Illness

- It is estimated that about 1 in 5 adults in the United States suffer mental illness in a given year (43.8 million people or 18.5 percent).
- About 1 in 25 adults in the United States actually experiences serious mental illness in a given year, in a capacity which is able to greatly interfere or limit one or more important life activities (9.8 million people or 4 percent).
- It is estimated that about 1 in 5 youth within the age range of 13-18 experience some form of severe mental disorder in the course of their lifetime. The estimate for children between 8 and 15 years is 13 percent.
- In the US, 1.1 percent of adults live with schizophrenia.
- Similarly, 2.6 percent of adults in the US live with bipolar disorder.
- About 6.9 percent (16 million) of adults in the United States have experienced at least one major depressive moment in the past year.
- Among the 20.2 million US adults who have experienced some form of substance abuse disorder, 10.2 million have actually had a co-occurring mental illness (about 50.5 percent) (SAMHSA, 2014).
- An estimate of about 18.1 percent of adults in the United States have experienced some form of anxiety disorder, such as obsessive-compulsive disorder, specific phobias, and posttraumatic stress disorder (PTSD), (National Institute of Mental Health, 2017).

Social Stats

Let's take a look at some recent social statistics, all based in the United States, revealing the level of impact mental illness has on our society:

- It is estimated that about 21 percent of local jail prisoners, as well as 20 percent of state prisoners, have recent history of a mental health condition (Glaze, L.E. & James, D.J. 2006).

- Only a little more than half the total population of American children (50.6 percent) between ages of 8 and 15 years old, with have a recognized mental health condition, have received mental health services within the previous year (National Institute of Mental Health, 2017).

- It is estimated that 26 percent of all homeless adults that are living in various shelters actually live with a serious mental illness, while 46 percent of all homeless adults actually live with substance use disorders and/or severe mental illness (HUD, 2010).

- In the past year, only 41 percent of adults in the United States who have some form of mental illness actually received mental health services. Additionally, 62 percent of the adults having a serious mental illness received mental health services in the past year (SAMHSA, 2014).

- An estimate of 70 percent of youth in the juvenile justice system have at least some form of mental health condition, while those who live with a serious mental illness are an estimate of 20 percent (NCMHJJ, 2007).

- The rate of use of mental health services by Hispanic Americans and African American is about one-half the rate of Asian Americans and Caucasian Americans (SAMHSA, 2014).

- Three-quarters of all chronic mental illnesses begin to manifest at age 24, while half of all chronic mental illnesses start at age 14 (Kessler et al., 2005).

Even with the provisions of effective treatment, long delays are often experienced which can span for decades between the appearance of the first symptoms and when the time at which an individual actually receives help (National Alliance on Mental Illness).

Understanding Mental Illness

At this point, it's important to provide a good explanation of what mental illness is. Generally, mental illnesses are health conditions which involve changes in emotion, thinking, or behavior (in some cases it can be a combination of all three). Mental illnesses are linked with distress and/or issues functioning properly in social, family, or work activities. Presently, mental illness in the United States is common. The following data is in reference to yearly statistics:

➢ One in 24 US adults have serious mental illness (4.1 percent)
➢ Approximately one in five US adults experience some form of mental illness (19 percent)
➢ One in 12 adults have a substance abuse disorder (8.5 percent)

A good mental health actually involves effective functioning in various activities on a daily basis and this leads to:

➢ Healthy relationships
➢ Productive activities at work, home, and school
➢ The ability to adapt to change and to be able to handle adversity

To continue, mental illness has to do with all mental disorders that are identifiable and diagnosable, and such conditions involve:

➢ Distress and/or problems associated with functioning at work, school, or home activities
➢ Remarkable changes in emotion, thinking, and/or behavior

The foundation for human communication, thinking, resilience, learning, and self-esteem is good mental health. It is crucial for maintaining relationships, sustaining emotional well-being, and contributing to society (American Psychiatric Association).

Some mentally ill individuals experience moments of relative stability, and within such periods, the common symptoms are reduced and interspersed with cases of psychiatric crises. For others, they remain seriously ill and dramatically symptomatic for an extended period of time. In correctional facilities, the category of acute mental illness is often limited to conditions such as serious depression, schizophrenia, and bipolar disorder (Toch & Adams, 2002).

Types of Mental Illness

Many medical conditions can be classified as mental illnesses, however, there are select types often more common among inmates.

Schizophrenia

This is a difficult, complex, frightening, and debilitating disease that may include symptoms such as disordered speech or thinking (rigid and fixed beliefs that usually have no basis in reality), and hallucinations (seeing or hearing things that are not there). It also includes confusion, inappropriate emotions, lack of attention to personal grooming, and withdrawal (Toch & Adams, 2002).

One of the subtypes of Schizophrenia is paranoid schizophrenia which is characterized by extreme suspiciousness and delusions of persecution. Although a person with schizophrenia may be classified as being in remission or fully recovered, it is more likely that the person will neither be ill nor well. However, the person will still experience a great deal of difficulty in adjusting to life situations, and some overwhelming demands and challenges can drive an already susceptible person over the edge (Toch & Adams, 2002).

Clinical Depression

This is also another mental disorder that can be experienced chronically or episodically. It often involves symptoms such as profound feelings of hopelessness, sadness, and helplessness. Some psychotic features can also be noticed, such as delusions and/or hallucinations. Other types of mental illness in correctional facilities include bipolar disorder, which is often characterized by frequent, dramatic mood swings from depression, to mania and clinical depression (Drapkin, 2003).

Anti-Social Personality Disorder (ASPD)

This is perhaps the personality disorder that is the most prevalent among inmates. The major symptom of ASPD is a pervasive pattern of total disregard and violation of other people's rights (American Psychiatric Association, 1994). Anti-social personality disorder is very common among men and most people with this disorder are often difficult to manage in a prison setting. This is because such persons can be volatile, manipulative, disruptive, and are prone to get involved in aggressive confrontations.

According to the results of epidemiological research, it is estimated that only 15 to 20 percent of inmates have a true diagnosis of anti-social personality disorder if they are diagnosed using the DSM-IV criteria. However, mental health workers in correctional institutions are prone to over-diagnosing the presence of anti-social personality disorder and frequently use it as default diagnosis for people that seem to have some sort of mental issues but are not exhibiting an obvious Axis 1 illness. So, in some situations, a diagnosis of ASPD at this point becomes a moral judgment rather than a clinical one, and inmates with ASPD are consequently mislabeled and regarded as "mad" or "bad" (Human Rights Watch, 2003).

Borderline Personality Disorder

This is another common mental illness among inmates, and it is characterized by associated patterns of instability in self-image and relationships, and significant impulsivity that often starts in early adulthood. Individuals with borderline personality disorder are usually volatile: they experience extreme emotions and are usually prone to depression. They can be manipulative and difficult, and in fact, on occasion, they can resort to self-mutilation. There are indications from research results to suggest that one of the major causes of this kind of disorder is childhood trauma, particularly resulting from physical and sexual abuse. Additionally, between 70 to 75 percent of individuals diagnosed with borderline personality disorder were women (Sartx et al., 1990).

Generally, individuals with a personality disorder may appear "normal", and yet sometimes they may just be difficult, but regardless, the mental disorders are real. These mental illnesses drive people who have them to act the way they do (Jones 'El v. Berge, 2001).

CHAPTER 3:
Causes Contributing to the Increase in the Rate of Mentally Ill Prisoners

"Law enforcement officers, prosecutors, defenders, and judges — people on the front lines every day — believe too many people with mental illness become involved in the criminal justice system because the mental health system has somehow failed. They believe that if many of the people with mental illness received the services they needed, they would not end up under arrest, in jail, or facing charges in court. Mental health advocates, service providers, and administrators do not necessarily disagree. Like their counterparts in the criminal justice system, they believe that the ideal mechanism to prevent people with mental illness from entering the criminal justice system is the mental health system itself — if it can be counted on to function effectively. They also know that in most places, the current system is overwhelmed and performing this preventive function poorly."

-Criminal Justice/Mental Health Consensus Project
(Council of State Governments, 2002).

Criminalization and Incarceration of the Mentally Ill

There was a total of 744,600 inmates in various city and county jails across the United States in 2014. Since it was estimated that 20 percent of the inmates suffered serious mental illness, then inmates with severe psychiatric diseases in US prisons would have been about 149,000 in 2014. It is important to note that this figure has increased since 2014. So, the question becomes: why is the number of mentally ill inmates increasing despite various ongoing efforts to reduce it? Several factors contribute to the increase in the number of mentally ill inmates in various jails and prisons (Treatment Advocacy Center, 2016).

In essence, there is a poor awareness of the needs of the mentally ill individuals as well as low efforts to support them within the community. Even in places where there was sufficient community awareness, there was still a lack of proper treatment facilities for individuals that were deemed mentally ill. Consequently, more people became homeless while the basic survival needs of many were not met, leading to their involvement in criminal activities and encounters with law enforcement (Ruiz v. Johnson, 1999).

Generally, most mentally ill persons have a higher tendency to commit crimes and the higher the number of people in various communities remain untreated, the higher the chance is that they will have encounters with law enforcement. It is actually believed that mentally ill persons are 64 to 67 percent more likely to be arrested by law enforcement than people without a psychiatric condition (Mason, 2007). About 42 percent of all crimes committed by mentally ill persons are associated with symptomatic expression, while 30 percent of those crimes are deemed survival crimes. The smallest percentage accounts for those crimes committed with the intent of actual criminal behavior (O'Keefe & Schnell, 2007).

A majority of the arrests of mentally ill persons are generally for minor crimes, which can easily be explained by the nature of their illness rather than mal-intent. People with schizophrenia have a higher tendency to be arrested for drug possession, trespassing, drug sales, property destruction, battery, theft, and assault (Daifotis, 2018; Human Rights Watch, 2003). Since most mentally ill persons have a higher chance of having a confrontation with law enforcement, they may also be experiencing various social disruptions or psychiatric disruptions, ones associated with their kind of illness, which often triggers them to misbehave. When they finally get arrested, these individuals with mental illnesses are given a police record which serves to further criminalize their mental illness. If a secondary infraction or misdemeanor occurs with an individual, the police may likely choose to work with the criminal justice system rather than the mental health system (Lamb & Weinberger, 2005).

However, mental health professionals, law enforcement, and other stakeholders are concerned that the criminal justice system has turned a solution for mentally ill persons that are hard to deal with instead of being treated properly. This is indeed the cycle that has greatly led to the constant increase in the number of mentally ill persons being incarcerated in various jails and prisons across the US (Daifotis, 2018; Human Rights Watch, 2003).

Inadequate Resources for Mental Health Services

The resources available for mental health services are grossly inadequate in comparison to the increasing needs of individuals with mental illness, and this has also contributed to a great extent to homelessness, failure in academics, unnecessary and expensive disability costs, and finally, the incarceration of mentally ill persons (New Freedom Commission on Mental Health, 2002). As a result, many people fall through the treatment services net into the criminal justice system. Another aspect that needs to be mentioned here is the lack of resources for community mental health services which hinders the ability of courts, law enforcement, and jails to divert individuals with mental illness to the proper treatment settings rather than the criminal justice system (State of Maine, 120th Legislature).

There are thousands of mentally ill persons who are not helped or properly treated until their condition worsens to the extent that they end up being prosecuted for various crimes that they would not have committed if they were given access to medication, therapy, and other living facilities within the community (Voskanian, 2002). One of the disturbing aspects of this cycle is included in a report by mental health professionals stating that it is almost impossible to get these individuals admitted to various treatment programs or hospitals until their condition has worsened to the extent that they would have already committed a crime (Daifotis, 2018; Human Rights Watch, 2003).

In fact, the relationship between incarceration and deinstitutionalization is not just the direct movement of the population of mentally ill persons to the correctional institutions, but deinstitutionalization has created so many problems, not just for the individuals that have been deinstitutionalized, but also for those that cannot enter the institutions in the first place. Some professionals have used the term "transinstitutionalization" to refer to the issue of individuals having mental illness who are not treated until they finally end up being institutionalized in various correctional criminal settings (Human Rights Watch, 2003).

Challenges with Obtaining Court Orders

Another factor that has contributed to the increasing number of mentally ill persons in correctional facilities has to do with the difficulty involved in getting the necessary court orders needed to commit persons having a serious mental illness to mental health hospitals. In most cases, the courts only grant orders for involuntary commitment on the condition that a person has become a threat to himself or to other people. In addition, obtaining court orders is dependent upon the court orders ruling that someone deemed mentally ill is too mentally incompetent to stand trial, or by getting a verdict from the court identifying them as "not guilty by reason of insanity." Consequently, individuals who are severely mentally ill or even psychotic often end up in jail (Human Rights Watch, 2003).

There are also theories to suggest that certain changes in civil commitment laws in the past two decades have resulted in fewer and shorter involuntary hospitalizations. The laws added more stringent criteria which center on the level of dangerousness of the individual rather than the mental illness itself. In addition, managed care also had a significant effect on the amount of time that patients have to spend in the inpatient unit when admitted to a care facility. As a result, a significant number of mentally ill individuals are unable to meet the criteria for civil commitment and as a result, are allowed to remain within the general community. In most cases, they are unwilling or unable to get outpatient treatment, which increases the chances of them engaging in activities that may result in incarceration (Temporini et al., 2006).

Economic Factors

> *"The mental health agencies of the DHSS [Department of Health and Social Services] have received budget cuts impacting their service. It feeds the mentally ill into the Department of Corrections. It's still cheaper to house the mentally ill in prison than in a state hospital. As money is harder to come by for the DHSS, plans for handling that person, providing services to that person, may not take place. And it's then not unlikely for us to see that person with our system".*

> -Mike Robbins, former acting mental health director,
> Washington Department of Corrections
> (Human Rights Watch, 2003).

Another key factor that has contributed to the increase in the number of mentally ill inmates has to do with economic incentives. This may lead to states moving individuals who are suffering from a psychiatric or psychological condition into correctional facilities as opposed to the state hospitals. The financial burden on state hospitals between is between $90,000 to $100,000 yearly when taking care of each patient, while correctional facilities spend about $35,000 each year for the treatment of seriously mentally ill persons (Maue, 2002).

Consequently, even when the correctional facilities are not suitable for such individuals, it is still considered better than allowing the mentally ill individuals to become homeless in the community. This has also led to an increase in the budget of correctional departments in recent years, rather than state agencies saddled with the responsibility of taking care of social and mental health services. As a result, while these mentally ill individuals are having a hard time receiving the proper mental health treatment they seriously need, these individuals are also the ones who are disproportionately incarcerated (National Resource Center on Homelessness and Mental Illness, 2003).

Increased Rates of Recidivism

There have been several studies aimed at exploring whether a correlation exists between the inmate recidivism rates and mental illness. Following one study that reported mixed and inconclusive findings in reference to a potential relationship, another researcher decided to conduct additional studies seeking to disprove and correct the lack of correlation identified in the first study. The results of the study, which were published in the International Journal of Criminology and Sociology in 2017, came up with the following answers to three main questions:

1. **First Research Question-** Is there a negative, positive, or null effect between mental health diagnoses and the possibility of post-prison recidivism? Based on the results of these findings, it was discovered that a major positive association exists between any mental health diagnosis (especially serious mental illness diagnoses) and the chances of recidivism after the release of inmates.

2. **Second Research Question-** Does a mental health diagnosis differentially possess an effect on various measures of recidivism, first in terms of re-arrest, then re-incarceration, and re-conviction? Based on the survival analysis of the data collected by the research team, similar effects were found across the three forms of recidivism results for both independent variables- any mental health diagnosis as well as a serious mental health diagnosis. However, the connection with the diagnosis of serious mental illness was significant only for re-conviction and re-arrest.

3. **Third Research Question-** Does a mental health diagnosis differentially affect the timing of recidivism? Based on the clear and distinct association that was discovered in all the survival

analysis models, there are indications that the presence of any mental illness, especially a serious mental illness, increased the chances of recidivism by an offender after being released.

4. **Fourth Research Question**- Are all offenders suffering from a serious mental illness, such as a Bipolar Disorder, Major Depressive Disorder, Psychotic Disorder and Schizophrenia, more, less, or no more likely to recidivate in comparison to other offenders having a mental illness that is less serious? Based on the survival models as well as the logistic regression models, there are indications that those diagnosed with a serious mental illness and not just any mental diagnosis have a greater likelihood of recidivating and often do so sooner.

In conclusion, the answers to all the four research questions reveal that mental illness among prisoners increases an individual's chances to recidivate (Bales et al., 2017).

Generally, mentally ill offenders often find it difficult to maintain a job or even get permanent housing. Since they have been sheltered, fed, and treated in the correctional institution, it is often difficult for released inmates to find a good job or housing. Landlords often feel reluctant to allow individuals with severe mental illness to rent their property and when they lack housing, adequate treatment, and a decent job, then their chances of recovery are significantly diminished. Also, their inability to live a normal life amongst society is dangerous to society, too, which contributes to an individual ending up in the hopeless cycle previously mentioned where individuals finally end up in jail, again (Gerstein, 2016).

CHAPTER 4:
The Effects of Mental Health Issues in Prisons

The practice of putting mentally ill persons in jails and prisons was initially practiced in the United States beginning in the mid-nineteenth century, but it was abandoned for various reasons. Although the practice has now been re-adopted, the major negative effects of the practice have yet to be resolved. This chapter will look to explore some of the negative effects of keeping individuals, who have a serious mental illness, in prisons.

Overcrowding: A Major Contributor

As mentioned in chapter three, there is a higher tendency for mentally ill inmates to return back to jail after being released. They remain in jail much longer than other inmates since their chances of obtaining bail are slim. In addition, they are more likely to violate the prison rules which further reduces their chances of obtaining a reduction in their sentence for good behavior. For instance, it is estimated that in Florida's Orange County Jail, inmates stay in jail for an average of 26 days, however, the average mentally ill inmate stays for 51 days. Additionally, in a study that was aimed at exploring the level of violation of prison rules by inmates, it was discovered that mentally ill inmates in jail were twice as likely to be charged with the violation of facility rules (19 percent vs. 9 percent). They actually accounted for 41 percent of infractions recorded in Washington State prisons, even when they only made up 19 percent of the population of inmates in the prison (Turner, 2007; Butterfield, 2003; Connolly, 2011 and Criminal Justice/Mental Health Consensus Project).

Wasting of Available Resources

Although there are several effective treatments for different mental disorders, they are often wasted in expensive interventions that are ineffective, and in most cases, such interventions only reach a small number of those in need. It is also believed that establishing separate psychiatric prison hospitals is not really cost-effective since maintaining them is quite expensive and their capacity is usually limited. Such psychiatric prison hospitals often have low release rates and when such individuals are released, they are left with a persistent and severe stigma. Some of these hospitals operate outside of health departments that are saddled with the responsibility of controlling the quality of the health interventions and there is presently insufficient evidence to suggest that such expensive psychiatric prison hospitals improve treatment outcomes (WHO).

Worsening Health Conditions While in Jail

Worsening health conditions occur often, especially in situations where inmates are not properly treated. Inmates who remain untreated usually turn out more symptomatic while being imprisoned. In most correctional facilities, mentally ill inmates are given the option to reject medications (unless in exceptional circumstances) which can lead to major consequences. First, correctional officers are prone to legal action in several states when they medicate mentally ill inmates forcefully, without their consent, and at the same time, they can even be held legally responsible for the consequences of an inmate's psychotic episode. This kind of situation is seriously unfair and wildly dangerous, both to the correctional officers as well as the mentally ill inmates (Treatment Advocacy Center, 2014).

A good example of such a situation is that of the self-mutilation by mentally ill inmates in correctional facilities. This includes the case of Michael Schuler in 2013. Schuler had taken methamphetamine because he was psychotic, and then with the aid of a pencil, stabbed out both of his eyes in Hennepin County Jail. He had been previously observed doing other things such as standing naked in his cell, screaming incoherently, and even standing on his own feces. He refused to take any medication (Lyden, 2012).

This incidence and several others serve to illustrate the challenges that correctional officers face in jails and prisons on a regular basis. Mr. Schuler was not being treated because he refused to be voluntarily medicated, which was likely the reason why a lawsuit was brought forth by him. Simultaneously, his reasoning for having blinded himself was that he was not given any medication, which prompted him to sue the jail for "providing negligent care when he was suffering from mental illness." So, correctional officers are often blamed if they act in such circumstances and are also blamed if they fail to act (Treatment Advocacy Center, 2014).

More Expensive for the County and State

As earlier mentioned, mentally ill inmates spend more time in jail than other inmates, which also suggests that they cost more to incarcerate. The extra cost of imprisoning mentally ill inmates is as a result of several factors. Some of the costs are incurred while taking care of their medication, while there is also the increasing expense of lawsuits that are brought against the county jails. Medication costs in the Iowa prison system, for instance, were estimated to have experienced a 28-fold increase between 1990 and 2000. In Washington state prisons in 2009, the most seriously mentally ill inmates cost $101,653 each when compared to about $30,000 yearly for other inmates. This cost excludes the increasing cost of lawsuits brought against county jails. For instance, the family of a 65-year old mentally ill stockbroker in New Jersey brought a lawsuit in 2006 against the Camden County Jail. The inmate was actually stomped to death while in jail (Miller et al., 2007; Bender, 2003; Rathbun, 2009; and Gottschlich et al., 2002; Lund et al., 2002).

One of the more extreme examples includes the litigious case of

Lamont Cathey, an inmate of the Cook County Jail. First arrested in 2015, Cathey was estimated to have cost Cook County Jail over one million dollars when, after being unable to post bail, began eating screws, metals, paddings, needles, and such, that then led to him needing multiple operations. Between the hospital bill and the 24/7 monitoring needed to protect Cathey from further harming himself, the cost of his incarceration increased tenfold. The costs continued to increase in 2018 when Cathey was arrested for a parole violation and spent three months in handcuffs in a private patient room at Loyola University Medical Center, estimating another total cost of $500,000 (Crepeau, 2018).

Some people are of the view that the family of the mentally ill inmate should be allowed to provide medication, which is actually permitted in some facilities. However, this also comes with the risk of illegal drugs being smuggled into the correctional facility, and in the event that something goes wrong, the jail or prison could be held responsible for any consequences. These are some of the reasons why this practice has not been allowed in many jurisdictions. Interestingly, if the inmates who are mentally ill fail to get medication, the jail or prison still has the potential to be sued which places the correctional institution in an unfair position of being sued regardless of what happens (Treatment Advocacy Center, 2014).

They Cause Serious Behavioral Problems in Correctional Facilities

Correctional facilities are known for being unpleasant environments on a daily basis as it is, but when they become overcrowded institutions with several persons loudly hallucinating and experiencing other symptoms, then they will become living hells. In several correctional facilities, such as one Oklahoma prison, it has been reported that things such as moaning, screaming, and chanting are normal and the level of noise actually increases when the sun goes down. A wide range of situations are included in this, for example when an inmate may believe that he's presently being held in a prisoner of war (POW) camp in Vietnam while another inmate will be screaming of a possible communist attack to take over the facility. As clearly stated by a deputy at Mississippi's Hinds County Detention Center:

> *"They howl all night long. If you're not used to it, you end up crazy yourself." One inmate even. "tore up a damn padded cell that's indestructible, and he ate the cover of the damn padded cell. We took his clothes and gave him a paper suit to wear, and he ate that. When they fed him food in a Styrofoam container, he ate that. We had his stomach pumped six times, and he's been operated on twice."*

(Fields, 2006; and Parker, 2010)

Leads to Increased Suicide Rates in Jails

Suicides in correctional facilities often happen disproportionately among mentally ill inmates. A study that was carried out in the King County Washington jail system of a total of 132 suicide attempters disclosed that 77 percent of the inmates who attempted suicide had a "chronic psychotic problem" when compared to 15 percent of such cases among the rest of the population in the correctional facility. One striking fact that was discovered was that a history of the abuse of substances was not more prevalent among those inmates who attempted suicide when compared with other inmates in the prison population (Goss et al., 2002).

Obviously, one of the greatest challenges that jail staff experience is the threat of suicide by inmates. This has led to the careful screening of newly admitted inmates for the possible potential of committing suicide. It has also led to putting in place an effective watch for inmates at greater risk. This leads to further issues, first of which is that the inmates would have to be monitored at least every 15 minutes or watched continuously, which is not an easy task. In addition, this extra care and observation will require more personnel, and this perhaps explains why the cost of taking care of mentally ill inmates is much higher than the cost of taking care of other inmates. The more frequent cases of suicide are a common cause of several lawsuits that have been brought against jails and prisons, which also results in higher costs (Treatment Advocacy Center, 2014).

Increases in Solitary Confinement

Keeping inmates in solitary confinement means that they will remain in a cell all by themselves for 23 hours a day. This allows the inmates just one hour to exercise and shower all by themselves. There are limited human interactions and the meals are passed into the cell by correction staff. With the increasing number of mentally ill inmates in various correctional institutions across the United States, there is also an increasing number of these inmates in solitary confinement. In 2003, it was estimated in New York prisons that about one-quarter of inmates in solitary confinement were mentally ill and in 2013, inmates with moderate to severe mental illness in Colorado prisons were believed to make up most of the inmates in solitary confinement (Zielbauer, 2003 & Brown, 2013). Most of the time, inmates with mental illness who refuse to take medication are kept in solitary confinement for two main reasons: they are either very disruptive or they are being protected (Belluck, 2007).

Increased Vulnerability to Victimization

Inmates suffering from mental health illnesses are disproportionately beaten, abused, and in some cases raped more frequently than other inmates. In a 2007 prison survey, it was disclosed that about one out of 12 inmates having a mental disorder reported at least one incidence of sexual victimization by other inmates within a period of six months when compared to one in 33 male inmates who have no mental disorder. The difference among female inmates that were mentally ill was three times higher than among male mentally ill prisoners (Dearen, 2005 & Wolff et al., 2007).

The Prison Rape Elimination Act was passed in 2003 by Congress and subsequently, the National Prison Rape Elimination Commission carried out a five-year study in order to investigate the issue. *In 2009, the report that was released provided indications that having a serious mental illness was a great risk factor for prison rape as well as in jails.* For instance, Joaquin Cairo was diagnosed with schizophrenia in 2013 and was arrested for criminal mischief. He was admitted to the psychiatric unit of Dade County Jail in Miami and suffered a fractured pelvis when he was violently slammed into a bed by another inmate who attempted to rape him. He subsequently died from the injuries inflicted in the attack (Ovalle, 2013).

There is a high rate of success by forensic hospitals in preventing mentally ill persons from going back to crime when they treat offenders found not guilty as a result of insanity. There is proof to establish that treatment of mentally ill offenders works, however the continued practice of putting mentally ill persons in the correctional institutions for various reasons such as the cost of care and the stigma of society has failed to stop the increasing number of mentally ill inmates (Byron, 2014).

There are some implications of using jail diversion services for mental health professionals, such as educating them on how to collaborate with law enforcement personnel. It also includes education on the integration of substance abuse and mental health services into the criminal justice system even with the segregated funding streams, as well as follow up that intensively monitored persons are given proper treatment (Okasha, 2004).

Some communities are making efforts to prevent individuals with mental illness from entering the criminal justice system in the first place with the help of specialized police or court-based diversion programs. While awareness regarding the increasing rate of incarceration of mentally ill persons increases, it is believed that individual communities will have to look at ways to expand available local resources for the treatment of mentally ill persons (Lewis, A).

CHAPTER 5:
The Negative Impacts of Solitary Confinement

"It's a standard psychiatric concept, if you put people in isolation, they will go insane.... It's a big problem in the California system, putting large numbers in the [secured housing units, California's supermax confinement facilities]... Most people in isolation will fall apart."

— Sandra Schank, staff psychiatrist, Mule Creek State Prison, California (Human Rights Watch, 2002)

One of the recent developments in correctional facilities is the use of solitary confinement by correctional officers in dealing with inmates who are considered dangerous or particularly difficult to handle. The continuous placement of inmates in solitary confinement, which sometimes lasts for several years, often leads to serious mental illness as a result of intense isolation. Consequently, the conditions of the solitary confinement incarcerations also have the capacity to worsen present symptoms and can leading to a recurring need to place an inmate in one (Jeffrey et al., 2010).

There is no doubt that mental health professionals working in various US correctional facilities encounter ethically difficult issues emanating from dual loyalties to employers as well as patients, substandard working conditions and the tensions that exist between good medical practices and the culture and rules of the correctional institution. One of the new challenges that mental health professionals have recently encountered is the use of prolonged solitary confinement of inmates having serious mental illness, a practice which has become prevalent despite the potential psychological harm it can cause. It is quite difficult to overcome the impacts of solitary confinement, especially because psychological stressors like total isolation have been identified to be as clinically distressing as physical torture (Reyes, 2007; Basoglu et al., 2007).

Despite the negative impacts, the practice of keeping inmates in solitary confinement as a way of punishing and controlling dangerous and/or difficult inmates has been increasingly embraced by correctional officers in the United States (Jeffrey et al., 2010).

An Overview of Mentally Ill Inmates in Solitary Confinement

As stated earlier, there are many mentally ill inmates in solitary confinement, which is mainly attributed to their difficulties in adhering to strict rules within correctional facilities, especially when there are few resources to help them deal with their disorders. As a result of this, their tendency to break rules can lead to an increase in punishments, particularly when they are involved in disruptive or aggressive behavior. When inmates accumulate histories of infractions, they end up in prolonged duration of disciplinary or administrative segregation. Let's take a look at some facts about the placement of mentally ill inmates in solitary confinement:

1. The New York Correctional Association provided a report stating that 23 percent of all the inmates in special housing units (SHUs) are actually on the mental health caseload (Correctional Association of New York, 1988). Based on the results of its survey of a sample of inmates in New York's SHUs, almost one-third of inmates in SHU who are on the mental health caseload also have previous psychiatric hospitalizations. About one-half of the inmates suffer from depression and 28 percent of them were diagnosed with either bipolar disorder or schizophrenia (Correctional Association of New York, 1988).

2. In Oregon, it is estimated that about 28 percent of inmates kept in the state's intensive management units, which are the most secure facilities in the state, are also on the mental health caseload (Human Rights Watch, 2002).

3. Inmates who have discipline problems in the Special Needs Unit (SNU) for the seriously mentally ill in Pennsylvania prisons are kept in the SNU Disciplinary Custody cells. A visit by the Human Rights Watch to Graterford prison revealed that eleven out of the 23 inmates in SNU were in Disciplinary Custody and were kept in their various cells for 23 hours daily (Human Rights Watch, 2002).

4. In Washington State's intensive management units, 29 percent of the inmates exhibited some symptoms of mental illness and 15 percent of them qualified as seriously mentally ill (Lovell et al., 2000).

5. The staff at Indiana's Secure Housing Unit (SHU) in the Wabash Valley Correctional Facility in 1997, acknowledged to the Human Rights Watch that between one-half and two-thirds of its inmates were mentally ill (Human Rights Watch, 1997).

6. As of July 2002, 1,753 inmates or 31.85 percent of the administrative segregation population in California prisons were on the mental health caseload (California Department of Corrections, 2002). In Valley State Prison for Women, 29 of the 44 SHU beds (65.91 percent) and in Corcoran State Prison, 423 of the 1,400 SHU beds (30.21 percent) were inhabited by mentally ill inmates (Ibid).

Most independent psychiatric experts, as well as correctional mental health staff, believe that confining inmates for a prolonged period of time in social isolation, accompanied with reduced mental stimulation and idleness is psychologically destructive. However, the extent of how destructive it is greatly depends on several factors, such as:

- Each inmate's prior psychological weaknesses and strengths
- The absence of activities and stimulation
- The extent of the social isolation imposed, and

- The duration of the confinement (Human Rights Watch, 2003).

A variety of individuals are specifically susceptible to psycho-pathologic reactions to the social isolation and the reduced environmental stimulation that are part of solitary confinement. The study of inmates in prisons led Professor Hans Toch to conclude that suicidal inmates may be pushed over the edge, and inmates who are pathologically fearful can regress into a state of psychologically crippling panic reaction (Toch, 1975). Additionally, Dr. Stuart Grassian stated that "individuals whose internal emotional life is chaotic and impulse-ridden and individuals having central nervous system dysfunction" are not capable of handling supermax conditions. However, this classification of inmates are the ones who are the most likely to commit infractions which will lead to segregation and isolation (Declaration of Dr. Stuart Grassian).

What Leads to the Solitary Confinement of Mentally Ill Inmates?

Even with several changes and improvements in correctional mental health services (which are usually related to litigation and the development of standards and guidelines by the American Psychiatric Association (APA), the National Commission on Correctional Health Care (NCCHC) and other professional organizations) the health care services in a majority of the correctional facilities remain greatly inadequate. There is an insufficient number of qualified staffs, few programs, and few specialized facilities relative to the number of inmates in need of help (Abramsky et al., 2003).

Considering the budget constraints as well as limited public support for investments in the treatment of inmates (as opposed to their punishment), elected officials have actually been reluctant in providing the required funds and leadership that is required to ensure that correctional facilities are equipped with adequate mental health resources. In a survey, 22 out of 40 state correctional systems reported that they have insufficient mental health staff to provide adequate support and treatment (Hill, 2004).

The ability of inmates with mental illnesses to deal with the stresses of being incarcerated, as well as their ability to conform to the extremely regimented routine of prison life, is often significantly impaired. Consequently, they may display annoying, bizarre, and/or dangerous behaviors and they experience a higher rate of disciplinary infractions than other inmates. Correctional officers, rather than considering their state of health, deal with them just the same way they deal with other inmates, and when the lesser sanctions fail to curb the behavior, the mentally ill inmates are eventually isolated in segregation units even with the potential negative mental health impact of such a confinement. When placed in solitary confinement, inmates can remain there for an extended period of time as a result of their mental illness and inability to learn or the required behaviors that would release them from isolation (Abramsky et al., 2003 & Fellner, 2006).

In cases challenging the segregation of prisoners suffering from serious mental illness, arguing it as unconstitutionally cruel due to the psychological harm it can inflict on inmates, the US federal courts have either issued rulings or accepted settlements that precisely curtail the practice or prohibit it entirely. According to one federal judge, *"placing inmates that are mentally ill in solitary confinement is the mental equivalent of placing someone that is asthmatic in a room with insufficient air..."* (Madrid v. Gomez).

However, it's unfortunate to note that with the exception of a few correctional facilities that abide by the outcome of such litigation, inmates who are mentally ill are still frequently placed in solitary confinement (Lovell, 2008 & O'Keefe et al., 2007). Human rights experts and international treaty bodies, including the Human Rights Committee (UNHRC, 1992), the committee against Torture (UNHRC, 2006) & United Nations Committee Against Torture, 2006), and the United Nations Special Rapporteur on Torture (UNSRT), have come to a conclusion that solitary confinement may be regarded as cruel, inhumane, or a degrading treatment of people, which is a violation of International Covenant on Civil and Political

Rights (International Covenant on Civil and Political Rights, 2010). The supermax confinement of inmates in the US have been criticized because of the mental suffering associated with it. (UNHRC, 2006 & United Nations Committee Against Torture, 2006).

How Does Solitary Confinement Affect Mental Health Issues?

In most cases, mentally ill inmates are more likely to be guilty of violating the prison rules as a result of their unruly behavior, often a consequence or symptom of their mental illness. It is the primary duty of correctional officers to maintain the facility and ensure that it's safe and secure. So, any disruptive behavior (whether the result of mental illness or not) will cause inmates that are mentally ill to violate the rules of the correctional institution. This means that mentally ill inmates are more likely to be kept in restrictive settings (Parker, 2009; Soderstrom, 2007).

Being kept in solitary confinement can act as a trigger, especially for inmates who are struggling from a mental health condition. Considering the conditions of solitary confinement, such as limited provision of mental health care services, lack of privileges, and lack of human interaction, inmates are often prone to experience even worse mental health symptoms (Daifotis, 2018).

There are several ways solitary confinement can affect mentally ill inmates; let's take a look at some of them.

Solitary Confinement and its Psychological Effects

Although solitary confinement has a great and devastating effect on the mental health of offenders who are subjected to it, its impact is often compounded when prisoners are kept in solitary confinement partly as a result of their mental illness. Mentally healthy inmates actually experience what psychologists refer to as "isolation panic", which includes the loss of self-control, panic, and eventual breakdown (Smith, 2003).

Stuart, Grassian, a leading researcher on the effects of solitary confinement, came up with a classification for the psychiatric condition of inmates kept in solitary confinement, known as SHU syndrome. SHU, which was used to explain the constellation of symptoms that are exhibited by inmates exposed to solitary confinement, is characterized by continuous changes, such as:

- Affective disturbance
- Difficulty with concentration, thinking, and memory
- Having issues with impulse control, and
- The disturbance of thought content (Arrigo et al., 2008).

Some of the psychological symptoms resulting from placing inmates in segregation units include anger, depression, anxiety, cognitive disturbances, obsessive thoughts, perpetual distortions, psychosis, and paranoia (Smith, 2006).

Leads to Limited Privileges

The main purpose of solitary confinement was to serve as a punishment for inmates that were deemed uncontrollable. This explains the reason why certain restrictions are implemented to ensure that the experience is as miserable as possible. The various restrictions include challenges involved in obtaining some of the resources which other inmates can easily get, including:

- No work
- Solitary recreation
- Absence of religious programs
- No school (except for self-study in cell)
- Restricted shower schedule
- Noncontact visitation
- No group programs
- Clothing restrictions
- Eating alone in cell
- No (or restricted) access to phone, television, and radio
- Restricted commissary list

- No library/law library access, and
- No art or music programs (Beven, 2005)

Even the physical movement of the inmates in solitary confinement is restricted by the nature of the cell, since the inmates are shackled and restrained whenever they appear before other people. The absence of these privileges and freedoms contribute to an unpleasant experience for mentally healthy inmates, but such conditions are devastatingly detrimental when the inmates are suffering from mental illness (Arrigo & Bullock, 2007).

The diminished environmental stimulation as well as the lack of social contact with other prisoners are also additional negative consequences of solitary confinement. Humans are social creatures and in order to remain sane, we need some stimulation. So, such an environment that inhibits interaction with other people will certainly cause inmates to further mentally spiral and this could even be detrimental to an inmate's mental health when such an inmate is already suffering from a mental illness (Beven, 2005).

The Use of Force on Inmates in Solitary Confinement

In a bid to deter other inmates from engaging in similar behaviors of inmates already being kept in solitary confinement, correctional officers may make examples of these individuals through the use of excessive force on inmates in solitary confinement. In response to minor infractions, prison staff often make use of violent cell extractions which involves the use of shields, batons, rubber bullets, and Tasers to bring inmates out of their cells. Despite the various motivations that have the potential to deter inmates from being placed in solitary confinement, mentally ill inmates still have an increased chance of being placed in solitary confinement because of the symptoms of their illness (Arrigo & Bullock, 2007).

Poor Mental Health Services for Inmates in Solitary Confinement

The treatment and resources for mentally ill inmates in solitary confinement across various correctional facilities in the country is seriously deficient. Although mental health services for the general prison population is limited, it is often worse for inmates in solitary confinement. The number of staff available to attend to the large number of mentally ill inmates in solitary confinement are few. Consequently, many of them are either untreated or not properly treated, since in most cases, the staff dismiss their symptoms as manipulation in an attempt to leave solitary confinement. In addition, the physical design and strict rules of social isolation as well as forced idleness, preclude treatment measures. In fact, the same conditions that can worsen mental illness are the ones that impede proper treatment and rehabilitation (Human Rights Watch, 2003).

Extended Duration in Solitary Confinement

When a mentally disordered inmate remains acutely disturbed for an extended period of time, their long-term prognosis also worsens. The best chance for a healthy recovery is the rapid and intensive treatment of acute psychiatric disorders, which also helps to reduce long-term symptomatology and disability. The issue of mental breakdowns and disability in supermax units within correctional facilities is actually two-fold:

- The conditions of the solitary confinement of inmates have a tendency to exacerbate already existing psychiatric disorders, which can lead to decompensation in people who are psychologically vulnerable when they are under duress.
- The second aspect is that when inmates are continuously confined in these same conditions (especially when tangible psychiatric services are unavailable), the state and health of the affected inmate tends to worsen even further, and the long-term prognosis worsens.

The length of time most inmates spend in solitary confinement is often substantial; they don't just spend some days in the "hole", but rather, they spend years and, in some cases, decades, in segregation. Sometimes, they are released from prison at the end of their sentence. Also, administrative segregation can be indefinite, contingent on the "good behavior" of the inmate, but disciplinary segregation can be endless as a result of subsequent infractions. Mentally ill inmates often find it hard to achieve sufficient periods of good behavior that will ensure their release because their inability to comply with strict rules (which caused them to be placed in solitary confinement in the first place) will often lead to an extension of their time in segregation (Human Rights Watch, 2003).

Mental health professionals are usually unable to fully mitigate the harm that is associated with isolation. This is because the mental health services in segregated units are often limited to: psychotropic medication, occasional private meetings with a clinician, and a healthcare clinician carrying out mental health rounds which includes stopping in front of the cell and asking how the inmate is doing (Abramsky et al., 2003).

Other activities such as structured educational activities, individual therapy, group therapy, life-skills enhancing activities, recreational activities, and other therapeutic interventions are often not available as a result of the limited resources and the existing rules that require inmates to stay in their cells (Metzner et al., 2006). Just as the number and proportion of mentally ill inmates have grown over the years, so, too, has there been an increase in the segregation and confinement of mentally ill inmates.

CHAPTER 6:
Common Types of Mental Illness in Prisons

At any given time, the number of inmates in various prisons around the world exceeds 10 million, and over 30 million are circulating through the system each year. The prevalence of mental disorders investigated within the prison system is higher than the general population comparisons. Even though the extent to which correctional facilities increase the cases of mental disorders is unclear, there is a reasonable evidence of the low rate of identification and treatment of mental illnesses. There is an increased risk of inmates experiencing all-cause mortality, self-harm, victimization, suicide, and violence. One researcher has outlined some modified risk factors. Even with this development, there has been a limited number of treatment trials for psychiatric disorders in correctional facilities (Fazel et al., 2016).

Among the types of mental illness suffered by inmates, depression and bipolar disorder are the most common. The numbers are actually starker when parsed by gender: about 55 percent of male prisoners in various state prisons are mentally ill while mentally ill female inmates are at about 73 percent. The Urban Institute writes that "only one in three state prisoners and one in six jail inmates who suffer from mental health problems report having received mental health treatment since admission." However, the increasing number of "mental health courts" in the US can help reduce the number of sick inmates that are untreated (Khazan, 2015).

U.S. Department of Justice, Bureau of Justice Statistics 2007 / Urban Institute

Types of Mental Disorders in Correctional Facilities

Depressive Disorder

Depression actually happens to be among the most common mental illnesses in modern society. It is estimated that 6.7 percent of adults in the US suffer yearly from the symptoms of persistent sadness, hopelessness, the loss of interest and energy, and changes in their appetite (NIMH, n.d.). Despite the prevalence of depressive disorder in the US, the resources needed to properly care for individuals suffering from this condition is inadequate as a result of low funding (Treatment Advocacy Center, 2014).

Due to the inability of the health facilities to adequately treat mentally ill persons, other facets of society have been left to handle the problems, one of which includes the prison system. It is estimated that as of 2012, ten times the number of mentally ill persons were actually housed in correctional facilities in comparison to the number in asylums (Treatment Advocacy Center, 2014). Among the inmates who were suffering from mental illness, 22 percent met the criteria for Major Depressive Disorder (MDD) and the prevalence was even higher in women (Conklin, 2000).

As depression is already more common among females, incarcerated women were actually 50 percent more likely to experience depression than women who were not imprisoned. It was discovered that the separation of jailed mothers from their children was a major factor contributing to this number and younger women with no children seemed to have lower rates of depression than women who were parents. Also, other factors that have been discovered to influence the rate of depression in correctional facilities include the number of visits that prisoners received and whether or not the inmates participated in the activities that were hosted by the institution like Bible clubs and parenting classes (Conklin, 2000).

Some Symptoms of Depressive Disorder

There are several symptoms of depressive disorder but not everyone depressed or manic experiences all the symptoms. While some people experience few symptoms, others may experience many symptoms. The severity of the symptoms varies with different people and also varies over time. Some of the symptoms include:

- Feelings of guilt, helplessness, and worthlessness
- Persistent sadness, empty mood
- Loss of interest or pleasure in various activities and hobbies that someone once enjoyed, including sex
- Feelings of pessimism or hopelessness
- Finding it hard to concentrate, make decisions, or recall information
- Feeling "slowed down", having decreased energy and fatigue
- Insomnia, oversleeping, or early morning awakening
- Restlessness and irritability
- Loss of weight and/or appetite, gaining weight and overeating, and
- The thoughts of suicide or death and attempts to commit suicide (Psychology Today, 2018)

Bipolar Disorder

This is a severe psychiatric disease that is characterized by recurrent alternating episodes of hypomania or mania and then depression, which is also separated by euthymic periods that are variably affected by residual symptoms and dysfunction (Geoffroy et al., 2013). The lifetime prevalence of bipolar disorder is estimated to be 1 percent for all cases of bipolar disorder 1 subtype and when all bipolar disorder spectrum subtypes are considered, it may reach 6.5 percent. This means that bipolar disorder is a major public health problem. It has actually been identified as the seventh most common cause of disability-adjusted life years by the World Health Organization (WHO) (Murray et al., 1996).

Just like patients with other mental disorders, people with bipolar disorder are more likely to be victims of violence than to be the perpetrators of violence (Kamperman et al., 2014). Some of the poor outcomes of patients with bipolar disorder include imprisonment, repeat offenses, and criminal acts (Pulay et al., 2008; Grant et al., 2005; & Corrigan et al., 2005). The manic phases of bipolar disorder are associated with criminal acts and transgressions (Yoon et al., 2012) and are typically characterized by exalted mood, increased energy, and irritability (Thomas, 2004). Most times, these phases are characterized by megalomaniac ideas as well as feelings of omnipotence which could result in committing offenses or confrontations with law enforcement (Christopher et al., 2012).

In a study of 66 inmates diagnosed with bipolar disorder, Quanbeck and colleagues revealed that an estimate of 75 percent of the inmates had manic symptoms at the time the offense was committed (Quanbeck et al., 2005).

Post-Traumatic Stress Disorder

PTSD is a mental health condition often triggered by a terrifying event, whether something witnessed or something experienced. The symptoms may start within a month of experiencing or witnessing the traumatic event and are classified into four types:

1. **Avoidance-** This includes avoiding activities, locations, and individuals that serve as a reminder of the traumatic event.
2. **Intrusive memories** such as nightmares that are related to the traumatic event, as well as unwanted distressing memories of the traumatic event.
3. **Changes in mood and thinking** such as hopelessness regarding the future, having negative thoughts about other people, oneself, and the world, and finding it hard to maintain close relationships.
4. **Changes in physical and emotional reactions-** This may include symptoms like trouble sleeping, being easily frightened or startled, finding it hard to concentrate, and engaging in

self-destructive behavior like consuming too much alcohol or driving too fast. The symptoms vary from person to person or over time (Mayo Clinic).

According to findings by researchers, PTSD has been discovered to be more common among male prisoners than in the general population. Based on the data collected by the researchers, it was discovered that being imprisoned almost doubles the risk of a man suffering from PTSD. A common misconception that people tend to believe regarding those who suffer from PTSD is that only military personnel who have recently returned from deployment experience it, however, anyone can actually suffer from PTSD. What it really takes is any traumatic event or events, and should even taken into consideration as to how life in correctional facilities is often experienced, as it can be filled with traumatic events, too. By going through the results of a survey known as the National Survey of American Life, psychologists at the University of Wisconsin, Milwaukee (UWM) discovered a connection between PTSD and prison (Element Behavioral Health, 2017).

The research, which centered exclusively on African Americans, found that incarcerated African American men were twice as likely to have PTSD as those who were never incarcerated. While less than 8 percent of men that have never been imprisoned struggled with PTSD, 13 percent of men having PTSD had been incarcerated. Other studies have also recorded a higher prevalence of PTSD in correctional institutions than in the general population. Having a thorough understanding of the link between incarceration and PTSD is important for multiple reasons. Being aware of the increased risk of suffering from PTSD by inmates will help healthcare professionals in preventing conditions and treating inmates. The disorder is a life-changing disorder especially when it is not treated (Element Behavioral Health, 2017).

Schizophrenia

Schizophrenia is among the mental disorders that inmates experience. It is a mental disorder that causes people to interpret reality abnormally and it may lead to a combination of delusions, hallucinations, behavior that hinders daily functioning, and extremely disordered thinking. This kind of mental illness can be disabling and individuals who suffer from schizophrenia need lifelong treatment.

Symptoms of Schizophrenia

Some of the symptoms of schizophrenia have to do with cognition, emotions, or behavior. Although the symptoms may also vary, they often involve the following common ones:

- **Hallucinations-** These usually involve seeing or hearing things that don't exist. Yet for the person with schizophrenia, they have the full force and impact of a normal experience. Hallucinations can be in any of the senses, but hearing voices is the most common hallucination.
- **Delusions-** It has to do with having false beliefs that have no basis in reality, for instance, having the thought that a one is being is harmed or harassed, and feeling that certain comments are directed at oneself with no real such experience. Most individuals with schizophrenia usually experience delusions.
- **Abnormal motor function or extremely disorganized behavior-** This symptom can be identified in several ways: it could be shown in childlike silliness or unpredicted agitation. Since the behavior is not focused on any goal, it is often difficult to execute a task. It can also include resistance to instructions, complete lack of response, inappropriate or bizarre posture, and excessive movement.
- **Disorganized Thinking and Speech-** In some instances, effective communication can actually be impaired and the answers that people who suffer from this symptom give may be partially or totally unrelated to a conversation or question.
- **Negative Symptoms-** They have a reduced ability (or lack the ability entirely) to function normally. Individuals with schizophrenia may ignore their personal hygiene or seem to lack emotion. Individuals with this condition don't usually make

eye contact, hardly change their facial expression, and often speak in a monotone voice. They may withdraw socially or even lack the ability to experience pleasure (Mayo Clinic).

Causes of Schizophrenia

The causes of schizophrenia are still unknown, however, researchers are of the opinion that it has to do with a combination of various factors, such as brain chemistry, genetics, and environmental factors. Despite the fact that the causes of the mental disorder are unknown, there are certain factors that have a tendency to increase the risk of developing or triggering this specific condition. Some of these factors include:

1. An increase in immune system activation like inflammation or autoimmune diseases
2. A family history of schizophrenia
3. Certain pregnancy and birth complications like exposure to toxins or viruses and malnutrition which may negatively affect the brain development, and
4. The intake of mind-altering drugs during teen years as well as adulthood (Mayo Clinic)

It is estimated that between two to three thousand men and women in various correctional facilities across the United States suffer from mental disorders, and among the common mental health disorders often experienced are bipolar disorder, schizophrenia, and major depression. However, in various locations across the United States, the mental health services of many correctional facilities are crippled by understaffing, woefully deficient treatment plans, and insufficient facilities. Most times, inmates who are seriously ill get little or no reasonable treatment; they are usually neglected, accused of malingering, and treated as disciplinary problems. When there is an absence of the needed care, mentally ill inmates will experience painful symptoms and their conditions will deteriorate. They are afflicted with debilitating fears, hallucinations, extreme and uncontrollable mood swings and delusions. They mumble incoherently, huddle silently in their various cells and even yell incessantly (Human Rights Watch, 2003). Many of these conditions also contribute to either first time or repeat offenses within individuals, leading to their cyclical placement in the criminal system.

CHAPTER 7:
Effective Approaches for Managing Mental Health Issues

For over 200 years, it has been established that the solitary confinement of mentally ill individuals in correctional facilities is inhumane and associated with several problems. The re-adoption of the practice in the US in recent years is incomprehensible when taken into consideration with these findings. Correctional officers are required to take responsibility for a set of individuals who are no doubt the most seriously mentally ill persons, even when the officers did not sign up to engage in such kind of job. The prison and jail officials are not actually trained for the care of mental health issues, but they encounter severe legal restrictions in their ability to provide treatment for mentally ill persons and are still held responsible when things don't work out well, which inevitably happens under such circumstances (Treatment Advocacy Center, 2014).

The detection, prevention, and proper treatment of mental disorders, as well as the promotion of good mental health, need to be part of public health goals in correctional institutions and are central to good prison management. Even in countries where resources are limited, steps need to be taken to improve the mental health of inmates and correctional officers. Such steps can also be adapted to the political, cultural, economic, and social context within any country. The following seven sections are great suggestions to consider in order to effectively manage cases of mental disorders in inmates (WHO).

1. **Move individuals with mental disorders towards the mental health system-** The correctional facility is actually the wrong place for individuals who require mental health treatment, especially when considering the fact that the criminal justice system emphasizes deterrence and punishment as opposed to treatment and care. To achieve this, legislation can be introduced to allow inmates to be transferred to psychiatric hospitals or facilities at every stage of criminal proceedings (arrest, prosecution, trial, and imprisonment). Providing a mechanism that will divert individuals with mental disorders who have been charged with minor offenses before they get to prison will guarantee that they get the much-needed treatment they need, and it will also help reduce the population of inmates in correctional facilities. The law needs to strictly prohibit the incarceration of individuals with mental disorders due to the lack of mental health services available there.

2. **Provide staff training-** All those involved in the prison system, including correctional officers, administrators, and health workers, should be trained on mental health issues. Such training will enhance staff understanding of mental disorders, challenge stigmatizing attitudes, increase the awareness of human rights, and encourage mental health promotion for inmates and staff. One of the most important elements of the training for all levels of corrections staff should be the recognition and prevention of suicides. Also, correctional officers need to have more specialized skills in identifying and managing mental disorders.

3. **Provide inmates with access to the right mental health treatment and care-** The access to assessment, treatment and (when needed) referral of individuals having a mental disorder, including substance abuse, should be an integral aspect of general health services available to all inmates. The health care services offered inmates has to be at least at equal level to those in the community. This can be achieved by establishing regular visits of a community mental health team to jails, providing

mental health training to health workers in correctional facilities, or even allowing inmates to access health services outside the prison setting. Inmates who require specialist care, for instance, should be referred to specialist mental health providers where they can be provided with in-patient assessment and treatment. Also, primary health care providers in correctional facilities should be given the basic training of how to recognize, as well as manage, common mental disorders.

4. **Ensure the availability of psychosocial support and rationally prescribed psychotropic medication-** With the availability of appropriately trained healthcare providers, inmates should have equal access to psychotropic medication and psychosocial support for the treatment of mental disorders with others in the community.

5. **The provision of information/education to inmates and their families on mental health problems-** Inmates and their families need to be provided with information and education on the nature of mental illnesses with the goal of lowering discrimination, stigmatization, preventing mental illness, and promoting mental health. With good information, inmates and their families can have a better understanding of their emotional responses to imprisonment and provide practical strategies that will help them reduce the negative effects on their mental health and inform them about when and how to seek help for a mental illness.

6. **Promoting the adoption of mental health legislation to protect human rights-** Every inmate (including inmates with mental illnesses) has the right to be given humane treatment with respect for their inherent dignity as humans. The conditions of confinement in correctional facilities need to conform to international human rights standards. Mental health legislation will serve as a great tool to help protect the rights of individuals with mental illnesses, including inmates. Currently, in most countries, there are outdated mental health laws which are ineffective in dealing with the mental health needs of the present

prison population (WHO, 2005). Developing legal provisions that help to meet the modern needs will assist in promoting the rights of inmates, including their right to quality treatment and care, to appeal decisions of involuntary treatment, to refuse treatment, to confidentiality, to protection from torture and other treatments that are inhumane and cruel (this includes the abusive use of restraints, seclusion, and medication as well as non-consensual scientific or medical experimentation), and to protect them from discrimination and violence. The legislative protection of other basic rights of inmates, like their rights to have acceptable living conditions, access to open air, adequate food, contact with family and meaningful activity, are vital and can also lead to the promotion of good mental health as well as rehabilitation. It is also great to establish an independent inspection legislation mechanism which will help to inspect prisons and various mental health facilities so as to monitor the conditions of individuals with mental illness (WHO).

7. **The promotion of high standards in prison management-** The mental health of all inmates, including inmates with mental disorders, can be enhanced when there are appropriate prison management systems that protect and promote human rights. It is essential to give attention to areas such as meaningful occupation, sanitation, physical activity, food, prevention of violence and discrimination, and the promotion of social networks (WHO).

The North Dakota Strategy on Solitary Confinement

In the United States, there are over two million individuals currently incarcerated, a figure that is almost equal to the population of Houston. Thousands of those incarcerated serve their time in solitary confinement where they are kept in cells without windows for between 22 to 24 hours at a time. Some are kept there for some weeks while others stay for months or even years (Corley, 2018).

Solitary confinement is known by different names such as protective custody, special housing unit (SHU), the "hole," isolation and several others. It was designed to punish inmates who break prison rules and are disruptive. Also, by removing such disruptive inmates, correctional staff are able to keep the correctional facility safe by isolating the difficult or dangerous individual from the rest of the inmates in prison. There is a growing consensus in recent years that the practice of solitary confinement is ineffective and cruel and one of the states that is changing the way it was formally done is North Dakota.

Their "administrative segregation" unit, which was the name given to solitary confinement, has been moved to a different area. Initially, there was little contact between inmates in administrative segregation and corrections officers, and the isolation unit was just like many others (Corley, 2018).

The New Strategy (The European Influence)

Several changes have taken place in the correctional institution; inmates in solitary confinement are now provided more recreational time. Inmates spend several hours learning new skills and they focus on changing their behavior. The changes have been credited to Leann Bertsch, who is North Dakota's director of corrections and rehabilitation, as well as the president of the Association of State Correctional Administrators, the organization saddled with the responsibility of tracking how jail systems are reducing the use of solitary confinement.

She got her inspiration after making a trip to Norway which was organized by US prison reform groups. Bertsch noted that:

There's such an overemphasis on punishment and punitiveness. You know Norway talks about punishment that works and when they mean it to work, it's to actually make society safer by getting people to be law-abiding individuals and desist from future reoffending.

The North Dakota corrections officers met to find out how to implement this strategy more broadly in the US and worked to define what could actually get individuals into solitary confinement in the first place. Initially, there were several behaviors that could get an inmate into segregation units before, but that list was narrowed down.

Minor infractions such as talking back to prison staff were dropped and instead, they established a list of top 10 dangerous behaviors, which included using a weapon, serious assault, and murder. Additionally, the name of the segregated housing unit was changed to Behavior Intervention Unit (BIU). The structure of the cells were also changed; the BIU cell typically has a long vertical window which allows light in from the outside and a slot for food. It has a small metal desk, a metal toilet sink, and a seat. Surprisingly, the room has several electrical outlets and some inmates who own a tablet or a TV can actually keep it in the cell. The inmate, on reaching the end of the wing, can even see cars moving outside.

According to the Clinical Director, Lisa Peterson, the aim is to assist inmates to succeed after they leave prison, since it had been realized that the old strategy was not effective. She stated that:

The idea that somebody is just going to sit there and think about what they did and magically know how to handle a situation differently in the future is not accurate. So, we have to be pro-active in helping people know how to change.

The results of these changes have been phenomenal. When North Dakota started changing its solitary confinement practice in late 2015, they had between 80 to 90 inmates in isolation, however, by June 2018, there were about 20 inmates. In North Dakota, the average stay of inmates in isolation (with some exceptions) is 30 to 45 days.

In a bid to prevent incidences of suicide, inmates in the unit are allowed to undergo a mental health screening, in part to find out if the inmates have suicidal thoughts. Also, they are allowed to participate in group therapy sessions and to learn new skills, like how they can cope with anger. Correctional officers talk to inmates in an effort to know how they are doing as they make their rounds rather than just writing up an inmate for negative behavior. The prison staff also write *"positive behavior reports"* whenever they notice any positive activity. In the correctional facility, rapport and skill building are immensely important (Corley, 2018).

The Benefits of the North Dakota Strategy

Corrections officials in North Dakota have admitted that it may be less difficult to change the solitary confinement policy of prisons in a state with few prison gangs and a mostly homogenous prison population. Despite the reform efforts, officials in North Dakota say that there are some inmates who are too dangerous to completely eliminate segregated housing. The prison, according to Director Bertsch, needs to be about providing a chance for change, so the decision of North Dakota to limit the use of solitary confinement as much as possible and to use it differently makes sense (Corley, 2018).

Other Ways to Manage Mental Health Issues in Prisons

Apart from the North Dakota strategy, there are also other points that can help deal with the issues of mental health in prisons. Let's take a look at some of them.

Providing Acute Care Services

When compared with people in the general population, inmates may be viewed as less appealing, less cooperative, and sometimes, less "human." However, the U.S. courts have been able to clearly establish that inmates have a constitutional right to be given medical and mental health care which meets a minimum standard (Ruiz v. Estelle) without an underlying distinction between the rights to medical care for physical illness and its psychological counterpart (Bowring v. Godwin). This implies that clinical services have to be made available in the inherently coercive system of the correctional institutions without compromising its goal and the ethics standards of the providers, which is no doubt extremely challenging.

The treatment challenges that correctional institutions face, which is as a result of the increasing prevalence of seriously and persistently mentally ill persons in correctional facilities, will continue for quite some time. Therefore, it is important to know the best setting in which proper health care services can be provided. There is a need to take a look at the developing acute care psychiatric units present within correctional facilities by shifting state funds from the departments of mental health to the department of corrections (Daniel, 2007).

Many departments of corrections actually have an agreement with state departments of mental health for providing acute care, and this approach leads to several conflicts. First, it leads to expenses that are associated with transferring inmates multiple times. It leads to interdepartmental conflicts and issues with communication, which is inherent in the difference between handling patients and handling inmates. These kinds of conflicts often involve the level and type of care, admission criteria, the limitations in terms of what each system can and cannot do regarding supportive and ancillary therapies, formulary differences, and access to medical records. The benefit of using acute care psychiatric units in correctional institutions includes:

- Having a safe and correct implementation of specialized treatments, like involuntary medication administration that is consistent with Washington v. Harper criteria (Washington v. Harper) for inmates who are gravely disabled to the point of being noncompliant
- Safe and proper implementation of specialized treatments, and
- The proper implementation of therapeutic restraints and of seclusion

In the event that inmates require acute care, they should temporarily be transferred to the psychiatric wards of general hospitals that have the appropriate security levels (Daniel, 2007).

Open Formulary vs. Restricted Formulary

A significant component of the overall mental health care cost in corrections institutions includes pharmaceutical costs, and generally, they often increase by about 15 to 20 percent each year. Consequently, prescription drugs usually become the target of aggressive cost-cutting by private health care providers. One of the most common tactics used in controlling cost is establishing a restricted formulary of older generation psychotropic and generic agents that are less expensive, making them cost-effective, as well as the insistence that the psychiatrist preferentially prescribe medications from the restricted formulary rather than the newer and more expensive medications which are also included in the non-formulary list (Daniel, 2007).

Inmates experience an improved quality of life by taking newer medications, and such medications can help to lower the overall cost of healthcare by greatly reducing the duration of long-term hospitalization, reducing the indirect costs that are associated with the movement of inmates to DMH facilities, and lowering emergency admissions to psychiatric units. According to the "Massachusetts Biotechnology Council White Paper Executive Summary" on drug costs:

> Given that prescription drug costs (10%) are a fraction of health care spending in the U.S. (compared with hospital and physician care: 32 v. 22% respectively), targeting pharmaceuticals to restrain health care cost is questionable as a significant saving mechanism and may, in fact, cost the healthcare system dollars if it involves restricting access.

Establishing practice parameters as well as guidelines for prescription practice, stringent peer review (including monitoring long and short-term side effects), and proper quality assurance activities should be the preferred method of cost stabilization and control.

Create a Careful Screening of Intakes

Identifying potential problems when people enter the correctional facility is one of the most effective ways to reduce the problems that are associated with mentally ill persons. There are several screening techniques available, however, all the techniques need to include an assessment of suicide potential and the medication history of an individual. There are guidelines that have been established by the American Psychiatric Association for serving individuals who are mentally ill in jails and prisons as well as possible alternatives (American Psychiatric Association 2000; Metzner, 1993).

Cost Studies Should be Encouraged

Among the major reasons why state mental hospitals were closed, and the subsequent transinstitutionalization of mentally ill persons from hospitals to correctional facilities, is the belief that it saves money. The daily cost of caring for inmates in prison may appear remarkably less expensive than the cost of care each day in a state mental hospital.

However, several costs have been omitted in such comparisons and this includes the higher cost of caring for inmates who are mentally ill, the higher recidivism rates among mentally ill prisoners, the longer duration of incarceration of inmates having mental illness due to the time that is usually required to restore their sanity to the extent that they can now stand trial in a court of law, and the high cost of settlement and awards due to lawsuits after inmate self-mutilation and suicides.

Establishing cost assessments that can identify the comprehensive expense of imprisoning mentally ill persons will offer officials a more accurate basis for making treatment policies for mentally ill persons and help to unmask cost savings that are unrealistic. Generally, the least expensive option is to ensure that seriously mentally ill persons get proper psychiatric care within the community so that they will not end up in prisons.

For instance, one study in Florida, completed over the course of seven years, followed 4,056 persons suffering from schizophrenia or bipolar disorder after they were discharged from psychiatric hospitalization. Among those followed, those that remained on medication were remarkably less likely to be arrested and cost the state 40 percent less in total care costs over the seven-year period (Van Dorn, 2013).

Mandated Release Planning

A written plan for psychiatric follow-up needs to be developed for all mentally ill prisoners being released from the correctional facility. Available results from studies have provided indications that this is currently happening in just a small percentage of cases (Wolff et al., 2002). A recent study revealed that prisoners with serious mental illness who were released from jail with no follow-up treatment were about four times more likely to carry out another violent crime when compared to mentally ill prisoners who were actually treated following their release (Keers et al., 2014). Part of the plan should be the identification of an organization that is specifically in charge of the psychiatric care of an individual. Such responsibility could actually be assigned to the correctional institution or mental health center, along with providing funding to enable them carry out their responsibility. The main goal is to ensure that an organization or an agency should be specifically charged with the responsibility of carrying out a psychiatric follow-up and will also be held accountable for the patient (Treatment Advocacy Center, 2014).

Encourage the Use of Assisted Outpatient Treatment (AOT)

Although the assisted outpatient treatment (AOT), which helps to assure treatment delivery to at-risk persons with mental disorders while they continue to live in the community, is available in 45 states as well as the District of Columbia, it is grossly underutilized. Assisted outpatient treatment has been deemed by the Department of Justice as an effective and evidence-based practice for lowering the rate of crime and violence where it has been implemented actively.

When it comes to reducing the time individuals with mental illness spend in correctional facilities, AOT has also shown to be quite effective. A study of randomly selected participants in North Carolina reported that patients "having a prior history of multiple hospitalizations combined with prior arrests and/or violent behavior" witnessed a reduction in arrests from 45 percent to 12 percent in a year while participating in AOT (Swanson, 2001).

Also, the percentage of individuals who are mentally ill in New York decreased from 30 percent prior to receiving AOT, to five percent while in the state's "Kendra's Law" program, and the percentage of those that were imprisoned while on AOT decreased from 23 percent to three percent (Kendra's La, 2005). There was also a significant reduction in drug and alcohol usage during the court-ordered outpatient treatment in both studies.

Every recommendation for the improvement of the health condition of mentally ill persons starts with the general premise that they should be treated in hospitals rather than the correctional institutions. However, based on the present situation, it seems that the public mental illness treatment system is ineffective. So, having a sufficient number of psychiatric beds for the stabilization of individuals that are mentally ill is required. Also, there should be a fundamental realignment of the public mental illness treatment system to ensure that public mental health officials both at the county and state levels are held responsible for any failure of the treatment system (Treatment Advocacy Center, 2014).

CHAPTER 8:
Inadequate Treatment of Mental Illness

The mental health disorders that exist among inmates have consistently exceeded the rates of disorders in the general population, and prisons in the United States serve as the largest mental health service provider (American Psychiatric Association, 2012; Torrey et al., 2010 & Wilper et al., 2009). Even with several court mandates for access to proper health care in correctional facilities (such mandates are generally limited to "severe" and "serious" mental illness requirements in correctional institution settings), prisoners' access to adequate health and mental health care has been sporadic (Scott-Hayward, 2009 & Adams et al., 2008).

The treatment decisions made in correctional facilities usually depend on the available resources (which are already limited), public support of correctional treatment, and prison management decision-making (Scott-Hayward, 2009 & Adams et al., 2008). The reports of several studies reveal that at least half of male prisoners and up to three-quarters of female prisoners reported symptoms of mental health conditions in the previous year, compared with the 9 percent or less in the general population (Wilper et al., 2009; Eaton et al., 2008; and Glaze et al., 2013).

Such rates highlight the importance of access to mental health treatment for prisoners since lack of access to adequate treatment will have vital policy implications, especially when the financial resources for correctional intervention and treatment are limited. When inmates with mental health conditions are not treated, they may be exposed to a higher risk for correctional rehabilitation treatment failure, which will lead to future recidivism within the prison system (Torrey et al., 2010; Mears et al., 2012 & Baillargeon et al., 2009).

In one of the studies it was discovered that after an inmate's release from the prison, former prisoners that received professional diagnosis of any mental health disorder were 70 percent more likely to go back to prison at least once, in comparison to former prisoners who were not given a diagnosis (Baillargeon et al., 2009). Additionally, among former inmates that had been incarcerated previously, the recidivism rates were between 50 and 230 percent higher for individuals with mental health conditions than those without any mental health conditions, regardless of the diagnosis.

This chapter will focus on specific and important mental health service issues across the United States, which helps explain the level of the problems that correctional institutions are facing today.

Understaffing

The provision of effective mental health services is staff-intensive. There is a need to provide institutions with a range of mental health professionals, which includes counselors, recreational/occupational therapists, psychiatrists, nurses, and psychologists, if inmates with serious mental illness are to get the individualized mental health interventions needed to deal with their psychiatric needs (Human Rights Watch, 2003).

For instance, dangerous staff shortages in some of North Carolina's toughest correctional institutions have worsened even with the recent efforts by the state to deal with the problem. New data suggests that more than one of every three-officer positions were vacant in January 2018. The vacancies have increased sharply over the past year. A Republican, Justin Burr, whose district includes Albemarle, told one legislative panel: "They don't want to go; they are retiring. They are quitting. They don't want to put their lives in danger."

About 37 percent of positions at Lanesboro were vacant in January, an increase from the 22 percent of a year ago, according to the N.C. Department of Public Safety Records. An officer who wished not to be named stated that some correctional officers are working nine straight days or consecutive 16-hour shifts. She further mentioned that the prison is so short-staffed that two officers are sometimes left to take charge of supervising 200 inmates in the cafeteria (Alexander et al., 2018).

In Arizona, the state has a contract with a for-profit company known as Corizon Health to manage health care in state prisons, however, reports indicate that the company has not been able to fully staff a wide range of medical and administrative positions which potentially put the lives of inmates, as well as prison staff, at risk. The contract specified the number of medical staff that each state prison needs, but based on the statewide numbers from several months, many of the positions are woefully understaffed. In June, physicians were just 51 percent staffed and psychologists only 67 percent staffed (Jenkins, 2017).

Also, in 2017, the state prisons at Lewis, Douglas, Winslow, and Perryville (the women's prison) had no medical director. Mental health services are especially lacking, as the positions of Mental Health Director and Psychiatric Doctor are empty. To put the dangers of understaffing into context, Arizona prisons have recorded four suicides this year. When testifying for the plaintiffs at a recent hearing, Dr. Pablo Stewart stated that, "This understaffing directly contributes to ADC's high rate of suicide." He also mentioned that it was due to "chronic and severe understaffing," and the few mental health care providers presently have huge caseloads but lack the sufficient time to evaluate everyone properly (Jenkins, 2017).

The major reason why there is an increase in understaffing in correctional facilities is that the prison systems are funded for very few positions, and this funding hasn't increased with the surging increase in prison populations. Additionally, prison administrators are having challenges in employing workers to fill mental health positions because of several factors:

    a.   The low pay offered to prison staff

    b.   The nature of the work environment, which is usually unpleasant

c. The fact that correctional facilities are usually located in places that are out-of-the-way, and

d. Working in the corrections has been historically regarded as "low status" work (Human Rights Watch, 2003).

Poor Screening and Tracking of Mentally Ill Inmates

The process of identification of inmates with mental illness is the essential predicate for mental health treatment. Courts in the United States have repeatedly noted that the US Constitution requires adequate screening as well as monitoring of mental illness (Ruiz v. Estelle).

However, there is a problem with the screening and tracking of mentally ill inmates in many correctional institutions. At the point of entry into the system, inmates with mental illness are not identified, and therefore they are not treated. If they are identified after screening and placed on mental health caseloads, the data management systems of correctional institutions are usually inadequate to effectively track the services provided or to make sure that the records of inmates follow them whenever they are transferred to another correctional facility. To further this point, inmates who develop mental health issues after they are admitted are often not identified and therefore aren't placed on mental health caseload in a manner that is timely (Human Rights Watch, 2003).

The initial screening takes place at the point where an inmate is admitted for the first time to a correctional facility (whether in the transfer to prison from jail or when an inmate is transferred between institutions in some systems). This screening involves a questionnaire that the inmates answer. When an effective questionnaire is used, the administrative staff does not need to have much or any mental health training. *The prison personnel will likely have a fairly good rate of referring new prisoners for more-in-depth evaluations if the screening questionnaire is adequate and administered properly* (Human Rights Watch, 2003).

As stated by the Consensus Project, effective screening should enable a staff to determine which inmates might require immediate mental health attention within 24 hours or a brief, reasonable time frame of three to seven days. In case the results of the screening suggest that an inmate needs mental health treatment (for instance, if the screening reveals that the inmate has been on medication for mental illness or has been hospitalized previously for mental illness), the inmate will then receive a more comprehensive examination which will include an inquiry into mental health records as well as other important information (Appelbaum et al., 1997).

However, oftentimes the staff carrying out the initial screening and a more comprehensive examination are not given the results of the previous psychiatric assessments as well as the assessments made during the inmate's pre-trial incarceration or any psychiatric diagnoses that were carried out as part of the trial competency or insanity defense proceedings. Such previous psychiatric workups may in fact never make it to the correctional facility (Appelbaum et al., 1997).

Untimely Access to Mental Health Workers

The American Psychiatric Association (APA) has pointed out that "timely and effective access to mental health treatment is the hallmark of adequate mental health care" (2000). However, it also concluded that such access in prisons is hindered by delays in transmitting inmates' oral or written requests for care, and this is further compounded by the imposition of fees that deter or prevent inmates from seeking care and the allowance of unreasonable delays before outside consultants or mental health staff can see patients (Ibid.).

Some of the most common complaints that mentally ill inmates make is that they usually wait for days, weeks, or even months just to see mental health staff after requesting a meeting or to get their medications altered. Other factors explain why an inmate may find it hard to receive (or continue to receive) pharmacotherapy for mental health conditions. One of the reasons is that psychologists and psychiatrists who are qualified to properly diagnose disorders are not sufficient within the system and the screening tools often used in prison settings are not diagnostic tests (Hills et al., 2004). The purpose of such tools is to gauge the security risk of new prisoners at the facility (Scott-Hayward, 2009). Another factor which may limit treatment access only to inmates that have the most serious mental health conditions, is the continuously declining correctional budget (Adams et al., 2008).

Cases of Diagnoses of Malingering

No other syndrome is as difficult to diagnose yet as easy to define as malingering. It is often difficult to reliably diagnose malingered mental illness, and it will often require the psychiatrist to consider collateral data beyond the patient interview. Malingering is the intentional display of false or grossly exaggerated psychological or physical symptoms that are motivated by external incentives (Diagnostic and Statistical Manual of Mental Disorders).

Many seriously ill inmates are untreated or under-treated because correctional officers dismiss their symptoms as manipulation or fake. Fred Cohen stated that a high incidence of the diagnosis of "malingering" mental records is the "sign of a system in disrepair" (Written Communication).

There are no specific criteria for ascertaining whether or when an inmate's behavior indicates mental illness or not. Violent or disruptive conduct may be a sign of illness, or it may be a sign of unruliness. Also, a quiet and seemingly introspective behavior may be just that, or it might be proof of decompensation (Metzner et al., 1998).

However, the ability to determine the true state of the inmate's health is part of the mental health clinician's art within or outside the walls of the correctional facility (Kupers, 1999). Also contributing to this, security staff that has not received proper mental health training are usually quick to conclude that inmates are acting manipulatively or voluntarily when they act out. Unfortunately, mental health workers have a tendency to be too quick to see manipulation or malingering and often overlook real mental illness (Human Rights Watch, 2003).

Although inmates can often be manipulative and feign mental illness for various reasons (to change housing assignments, get a transfer, improve their legal situation or get attention), manipulation is usually not unconnected and unrelated to mental illnesses. While symptoms such as self-mutilation can be manipulative, they are also simultaneously a symptom of major psychiatric disorders or a self-reinforcing behavior that needs a psychiatric response (Human Rights Watch, 2003).

To enhance the recovery and alleviation of the symptoms of mental illness, mental health treatment in the community as well as in prison needs to include a variety of mental health therapies. It should be multidisciplinary and eclectic and rendered in a way that is consistent with generally accepted mental health practices (Ibid). The treatment needs to reflect an individualized, written treatment plan for each inmate who is identified as mentally ill, and factors such as psychiatric diagnoses (before and after incarceration), life history, and other factors should also be considered. Such treatments shouldn't be limited to alleviating immediate symptoms via psychotropic medication (Council of State Governments, 2002).

CHAPTER 9:
Poor and Inadequate Responses from Correctional Staff

Correctional officers interact daily with inmates, which means that they are handling a very difficult task in equally difficult circumstances and environments. Despite the insufficient number of officers employed in various correctional institutions across the United States, these officers are expected to exercise power over and maintain control of inmates in facilities that are overcrowded and devoid of opportunities to ensure that the inhabitants are peacefully and productively engaged. The frustrations and difficulties that employees face as correctional officers are even further compounded when inmates have a mental illness.

The problematic behavior of mentally ill inmates, who, on occasion, can be bizarre and aggressive, is capable of trying the patience of anyone, including mental health professionals. However, there are some correctional officers who have the right training as well as an understanding of the nature of mental illnesses, which help them cope well with the challenges associated with mentally ill inmates. During their training, these correctional officers learn the culture of obedience, order, and discipline, but it makes them ill-prepared for correctly dealing with inmates with behaviors that are either chronically or episodically driven by their mental illness (Human Rights Watch, 2003).

The Correctional Officers' Role

The daily contact of clinicians with inmates is brief when compared with the level of contact correctional officers have on a daily basis; they practically "live" with inmates 40 hours weekly in the housing units. The correctional officers are the first set of people to notice any significant changes in the routine or mental status of inmates. In a structured correctional facility, the bizarre behavior of an inmate who exhibits signs of mental illness, their increased aggressive behaviors, and the deterioration of self-care or irritable behaviors always tend to stand out (Appelbaum et al., 2001).

The mental health staff look to the prison officers to get this information, since the patients usually "appear clean and good" while in the clinician's office once every week, even when their general functioning is becoming impaired. The information obtained from correctional officers contributes to diagnostic assessments as well as the ongoing monitoring of patients. Additionally, in some cases, the mental health staff may inform security staff regarding patients that require special monitoring due to increased risk (Appelbaum et al., 2001).

Even though alerting security staff about an inmate's risks requires the sharing of confidential clinical information with the prison staff, the effective management of inmates with mental disorders supports this practice "whenever such sharing would facilitate the treatment or safety of an inmate" (Unpublished report to the Massachusetts Department of Correction, Appelbaum K, Dvoskin J, Geller J, et al., 1997). Correctional officers who have access to such information should be required to maintain appropriate confidentiality. It's also important to consider some of the roles of correctional officers in handling inmates with mental illness:

Intervention- Prison staff play a crucial role in the interventions that involve mentally ill inmates. A knowledgeable and concerned correctional officer can help an inmate who is functionally impaired by providing prompts or supports that will assist the inmate in meeting the demands of the correctional environment. The officers can also enforce the inmate's attendance at mental health appointments and encourage the inmates to comply with their treatment. They can also alert the health staff anytime they notice that an inmate has refused to take his medications (Appelbaum et al., 2001).

Specialized Programs- There are various specialized units in correctional facilities across the United States, which are usually called residential treatment units. These units were developed to house and treat inmates who are functionally impaired (Condelli et al., 1994 & Metzner, 1998). Such structured units usually have a low ratio of inmates to clinicians, and they work on inmates' behavioral changes by making use of group and occupational therapy models. In these residential treatment units, correctional officers who are stationed there play a crucial and unique role and function as part of the treatment team. Inmates receive coordinated and consistent care when there are regular meetings and discussions between the clinicians and correctional officers. When managing and curbing the maladaptive behaviors of inmates in the unit, the officers' authority to provide discipline as well as enforce sanctions becomes very important (Appelbaum et al., 2001).

Correctional Officers vs Mental Health Staff

Even though both employees need to work together cooperatively, they have distinct professional cultures and missions which should be recognized and appreciated (Faiver, 1998). The primary mission of the correctional officers is to serve society by confining inmates, while the primary mission of mental health providers, as well as other healthcare staff, is to serve patients by providing treatment.

When it comes to the correctional culture, this generally includes universally applied rules, regimentation, implicit authority of security staff, and the punitive sanctions for violations by prisoners. In contrast to the correctional culture, is the culture of health professions, which is characterized by informed consent, individualized treatment, and negotiated compliance (Appelbaum et al., 2001).

Several commentators have explained how the disparity in ideologies that exists between mental health staff and security staff often leads to conflicts between the two groups (Powelson et al., 1951; Cormier, 1973; Cumming et al., 1973; Kaufman, 1973; Culbertson, 1977 & Roth, 1986). For instance, some prison staff view mental health providers as gullible, excessively soft, and guilty of coddling the inmates. They view mental health problems as character flaws, and some officers even hate the fact that inmates are given access to free services which many people in the non-prison community lack. They also view mental health care as an undeserved (if not unneeded) service for inmates. Sometimes, correctional officers may even view their treatment as protecting inmates from the consequences of their own behavior (Appelbaum et al., 2001).

This bias is not only for correctional officers alone, because mental health care staff tend to perceive prison officers as being unnecessarily punitive and harsh toward inmates. They are of the view that the antisocial propensities of prisoners and their mental health problems are indications for treatment, not punishment. There are some truths in the perception of both professional groups. For instance, mental health care providers are sometimes naive and prone to excusing inmates' inappropriate behaviors. While in contrast, some prison staff are inappropriately harsh, but the blanket characterization of both parties does everyone a disservice (Appelbaum et al., 2001).

Abuse and Mistreatment in the Correctional Facilities

On April 24th, 2016, Terrill Thomas slumped over and died after staying in solitary confinement for seven days without water in a Milwaukee County Jail cell. His fellow inmates reported that he had been begging correctional officers to provide him with something to drink for a week. According to the testimony of the investigating detective, "Thomas asked every correctional officer for water because the water in his cell was shut off."

The investigation into this case is resulted in an indication of the level of abuse that is common in various prisons and jails across the United States. The distressing frequency of the degrading treatment of inmates still takes place. Take a look at the statistics regarding the cases of inmate abuse in New York State between 2010 and 2015:

- There were 120 abuse cases brought forth against correctional officers

- 80 of the abuse cases were settled with disciplinary action (no dismissal)
- 30 correctional officers were up for dismissal
- Only eight actually dismissed (Ptacin, 2017)

According to a Human Rights Watch report released in 2015, mentally ill prisoners in various prisons across the US are subjected to routine physical abuse by correctional officers. Details of the 127-page report reveal that correctional officers have "broken the jaws, noses, ribs of inmates leaving them with lacerations that require stitches, deep bruises, second-degree burns and even damaged organs. Sometimes, inmates were doused with chemical sprays, strapped to chairs or beds for days and shocked with stun guns" (Ptacin, 2017).

In several cases, such as Terrill Thomas' case, inmates have died due to the use of brute force, though the number of casualties remains unclear partly because correctional institutions classify them in different ways and often fail to report the abuse. According to Jamie Fellner, a senior adviser at Human Rights Watch who wrote the 2015 report, "Force is used against prisoners even when, because of their illness, they cannot understand or comply with staff orders."

Within 12 months, a National Inmate Survey, which was conducted by the Justice Department's Bureau of Justice Statistics, revealed that 4.4 percent of inmates in prison and jail reported being sexually victimized. The definition of sexual abuse by the Bureau includes physical contact as well as verbal abuse. However, it is extremely difficult to prove cases of verbal abuse, and such cases hardly result in the recovery of damages (Ptacin, 2017).

It is not uncommon for correctional officers to turn off their compassion and empathy. In a recent in-depth article, investigative journalist Shane Bauer worked as a correctional officer in Louisiana for four months, earning $9 each hour, and later found himself violent and fearful, wanting to inflict his rage on inmates (Ptacin, 2017).

Systemic Factors to Consider

Although there are laws and acts of protection in place as well as a great commitment by activists to prevent violence in prisons, these acts of violence will continue to exist for several reasons:

- Correctional officers are not earning a reasonable salary; the average hourly rate for a prison officer is $16.54 per hour.
- The prison officers often tend to receive sparse training and even less emotional support. Sometimes, these correctional officers who perpetrate the violence and harm are not really at fault; they are not properly trained, and they are made to take up this powerful role, which can be scary and violent. It can even be traumatic for individuals meant to enforce an order to observe or engage in the violence.
- The correctional facilities are overcrowded; they are usually packed beyond their capacity (Ptacin, 2017).

The training of correctional officers in mental health issues will support the officers in overcoming common assumptions, such as the idea that mental health providers and security staff are worlds apart in concerns, views, and strategies used in dealing with prisoners. When correctional officers and mental health professionals were interviewed by the Human Rights Watch, both agreed on the importance of mental health training for correctional officers. The professionals noted that training on various signs and natures of mental illnesses would enable prison officials to respond better to problems that occur with inmates and would empower them to properly assist mental health staff (Human Rights Watch, 2002).

Presently, such training is sorely lacking, though the results of a survey by the National Institute of Corrections indicated that 40 states claimed to provide health training for prison officers. However, the training was minimal. Ten correctional institutions claimed to include an estimate of four hours of mental health classes in their basic training package for new correctional officers. In addition to this, 13 admitted that they provided fewer than four hours, while seven states claimed to have provided over four hours of training (National Institute of Corrections, 2001).

Although it may be quite challenging to significantly reduce the presence of violence in prisons, certain things can be done to help inhibit the frequency of such incidences. One of the things that can be done to help support mentally ill inmates in prison is to pay more attention to incarceration policies and to pay attention to who the DA is that wants to run for election. Most DAs often run unopposed and are generally extremely conservative; they think that part of their job is to put people in prison, which is not true. They often over-charge and this suggests that they will end up sending higher numbers of people to prison in an effort to fill prison beds (Ptacin, 2017).

Despite the differences that exist between mental health providers and correctional officers in their mission, training, and culture, both have some common goals. Prison officials play a crucial role in the delivery of multidisciplinary mental health services in prisons and jails. When prison officers share the appropriate information with clinicians and also help in managing inmates with mental illness, there will be an improvement in the quality of treatment and safety of the correctional environment. Correctional officers can establish the foundation for meaningful contributions to mental health care by ensuring mutual respect, ongoing communication and cooperation, as well as proper orientation and training (Appelbaum et al., 2001).

CHAPTER 10:
The Impact of the Prison Environment on Mentally Ill Inmates

Mentally ill inmates are usually confined to the same prisons as other inmates, except when they are transferred to a hospital or an acute care setting. As a result of the massive prison building campaign over the past few decades, several states have decided to keep up with the soaring population of inmates, which came about because of prisoner litigation challenging the conditions of confinement. Most prisoners in the US are imprisoned in minimally acceptable physical facilities. This means that, at minimum, they don't live in vermin-infested, filthy, decrepit and decaying facilities without sufficient sanitary facilities, water supplies, lighting, and ventilation. However, there are still thousands of inmates who live in facilities that are seriously overcrowded, decrepit, poorly ventilated, dark and dirty. Many states are experiencing severe overcrowding (BJS, 2002).

Among inmates with mental illnesses, the risk of serious psychological harm due to poor living conditions is high. In Navasota, Texas, two aging inmates at the Wallace Pack Unit, Keith Milo Cole and John Wesley Ford, became bothered about how their prolonged exposure to arsenic-laced water as well as extreme heat during the summer months might have affected their health over a long-term period. Cole revealed that the color of the water found in his unit was brown, and as a result, a federal judge ordered the Texas Department of Criminal Justice (TDCJ) to provide inmates with safe drinking water. According to Cole, who is serving a life sentence, "It used to be where you could take a white wash rag and put it in the sink and water would run on it about 10 or 15 minutes, and it would actually turn brown."

The plight of inmates is an indication of a nationwide problem which is inextricably connected to the power imbalance that exists within the US criminal legal system (a legal system in which inmates are usually out of sight and therefore, out of public mind). According to a special investigation carried out by the Truthout and Earth Island Journal, the toxic impact of correctional facilities extends beyond any one particular prison or specific region within the US. Although there are correctional facilities that provide egregious examples, the fact remains that mass incarceration in the United States greatly impacts the health of inmates, the adjacent communities, as well as the local ecosystem (Bernd et al., 2017).

The Prison Policy Initiative revealed that there are currently 2.3 million people confined in over 6,000 jails, prisons and detention centers operated by the federal, state, county, and private sectors. Since the 1970s, the United States has experienced a 700 percent increase in the number of incarcerated persons due to an increase in the "tough on crime" and "war on drugs" policies. The rate of incarceration of people in the US is some five times higher than most countries around the world (Bernd et al., 2017).

Keeping a large number of individuals in closed facilities attracts several human rights issues as well as a host of associated civil rights problems. However, until recently, not much research had been made to unravel the connections between the mass incarceration of people and environmental issues, which has to do with the problems that occur when correctional facilities are located on or near toxic sites, as well as when the correctional facilities themselves become the main source of toxic contamination (Bernd et al., 2017).

What is the Level of Environmental Impact?

> *"It is just not feasible to expect individuals to become healthy in an unhealthy environment."*
>
> —(López et al., 2017)

The custodial nature of the correctional environment is antithetical to the therapeutic settings that are needed for inmates who are vulnerable, depressed, psychotic, or suicidal. In the current conception and design of modern correctional facilities, the focus is far behind the crushing complexities of mental illness. In fact, several mental health care professionals have labeled correctional facilities as "anti-therapeutic."

Prisons are generally recognized for their harsh and distressing social settings; they are not conducive to mental stability, let alone recovery. It's been demonstrated on several occasions that correctional environments can aggravate and as well as amplify mental health conditions (with the period of incarceration also having the potential to "heighten vulnerability and increase the risk of suicide and self-harm" (López et al., 2017).

Some of the common prison experiences inmates have include violence, overcrowding, enforced solitude, bullying, isolation from social networks, lack of any meaningful activity and the insecurity regarding prospects. All these factors coupled with other physical environmental factors such as bad acoustics, dark and narrow corridors, fluctuations in temperature, limited natural light, and lack of privacy are all counterproductive to the therapeutic conditions that are required for mental health and rehabilitation. As a result of this unforgiving climate, many inmates who are mentally unstable are sent on a downward spiral, which consequently makes attempts at recovery a distant possibility. Most of these conditions are not the fault of the prison administrators; the correctional facilities lack adequate funding, and the physical plants are outmoded and were built in a different era (López et al., 2017).

The Effects of Staff Shortage on Working Environment and Culture

Part of the problem that leads to a poor environment in correctional facilities has to do with the reduction in the number of staff members in prisons. This reduction in staff numbers, as well as the concurrent increase in the number of inmates over the past few years, has been perceived as a significant cause of stress among staff as well as inmates. Consequently, inmates no longer have much time to spend outside their cells since there are fewer members of staff left to supervise them. This increases tensions between inmates and correctional officers. Factors such as poor management style, less job satisfaction for officers, insufficient information, lack of communication, and lack of continuity of care, were identified as the causes of increased stress levels among officers (Nurse et al., 2003).

Based on a study to discover the influence of environmental factors on the mental health of individuals within correctional facilities, there are indications that wider environmental and organizational factors affect mental health within correctional institutions. The data obtained from the study revealed that when inmates are locked up without access to mental stimulation, it negatively impacts their mental health status, regardless of whether they had a formal mental illness or not. Additionally, the reduction in staff levels resulted in more stress for the remaining staff members. This shortage also led to longer lock-up times for inmates, which in turn, affected their mental health (Nurse et al., 2003).

Characteristics of an Ideal Prison Environment for Mentally Ill Inmates

There are several characteristics of a therapeutic and healing environment, which is ideal for mentally ill inmates:

1. **The environment should be supportive and nurturing** - Healing takes place through healthy relationships and meaningful sharing. An environment that is supportive and nurturing promotes various positive human interactions as well as values like trust, empathy, and hope, values that are essential to treatment. In a benevolent environment, the emotional, physical, and spiritual needs of the residents are identified, respected and met by the correctional officers. In such environments, the correctional officers are enthusiastic about transforming the lives of inmates and it is expected that

they foster stronger relationships and spend more time inter-acting with residents. They also encourage inmates to attend therapy groups or simply check on them while offering a compassionate voice. The design of this kind of facility should minimize the barriers that exist between the inmates and staff. The barrier or separation of inmates from staff should only be based on documented levels of risk.

2. **An environment that does no harm** - The main cause of psychiatric or psychological distress for many people (especially youth and females) relates to some form of past trauma. This could be emotional or physical abuse, violence, neglect, etc. An environment that meets the basic needs for physical safety and security is a very important aspect of trauma-informed design. This includes predictable spaces and clear sightlines all throughout the facility, with no blind spots, and rather than edges on furniture and other surfaces, it should be curvilinear. Operationally, the safety of such facilities is accomplished via a dynamic security approach which promotes and sustains normalized communication between inmates and staff.

3. **An environment that is calming and comfortable** - The prison facility should be a calming and comfortable environment, which can be achieved with nature views, selective colors, texture, furnishing, and materials. The addition of certain aspects of nature into the design of an ideal prison environment that is therapeutic, is known to lower aggression and stress in inmates. Introducing nature into space in the correctional facility involves introducing certain features such as open recreation, which has seating areas, small courtyard gardens, plants, etc. The facility needs good air quality; extreme temperature fluctuations are not comfortable, rather, they are confusing to inmates with mental illness. Individuals with brain disorders are not comfortable in places with hard concrete spaces because they create disturbing noise levels. They require environments that are more natural and softer, which can help de-stress the environment. Since therapy is usually based on verbal

communication as well as the privacy of the patients, it's important to control the sound levels in mental health settings.

4. **A normalized environment**- An environment which will reflect the real situations that residents will meet after spending their time in prison only serves to help adapt them to society in preparation for their departure. The prison environment should, as much as possible, strive to provide the inmates with a sense of normalcy based on the fact that correctional facilities that look like the world outside have given an indication that it provides inmates a better chance of reintegrating into society successfully when they are released (López et al., 2017).

A Specialized Unit for Mentally Ill Inmates

Many correctional facilities in different countries around the world lack the right strategies to identify, separate, and properly treat inmates suffering from mental health issues: "When the mentally ill are treated the same as the non-mentally ill criminal population, there is no difference in housing or treatment," said Margaret Bower.

Consequently, there is a lack of specialized housing accommodations, as well as services, for inmates who are mentally ill in correctional facilities internationally. Although not all mentally ill inmates need specialized housing while in prison, some inmates require a higher level of care (acute and sub-acute populations) and the prison needs to be ready to deal with their needs or face the risk of the prisoners' further decomposition and/or victimization. Both healthcare and correctional professionals agree that when prison management is facilitated, the outcomes are better when housing is differentiated for prisoners having serious mental health issues. The type of accommodation for mentally ill inmates can vary based on the seriousness of the mental disorder (López et al., 2017).

Based on a person-centered medical and psychological approach, inmates should be assigned to the proper living unit and level of supervision which has the least restrictive response that is appropriate to the classification risk. The major challenge that architects face is security, and it should be handled in a similar way to the designing of a mental health facility in a non-correctional setting.

It is recommended that inmates who exhibit symptoms of acute mental health disorders should be placed in single cells, because they will have fewer disruptions and cases that often occur in multi-occupancy cells. Single cells can help to promote an environment that is quiet which helps mentally ill inmates to sleep well and lower their levels of agitation. The double bunk with other patients is more appropriate for the sub-acute populations, as health allows. For inmates who are transitioning back to the general population, multi-occupancy, double bunk (4-person alcoves) or open dormitory configurations can be used. However, this will depend on the standard accommodation that is applied to the general population, based on classification and security levels, which differs among countries (López et al., 2017).

Examples of facilities that demonstrate this concept include:

- The proposed New Health Services Building in Austin, Texas. Travis County Correctional Complex, Austin, TX CGL Planning and Architecture, which has Adult Correctional Facilities Master Plan, now includes a new 468-bed Health Services Building that will provide a variety of cell typologies as well as housing units for male and female prisoners in all the identified mental health needs category.
- California Health Care Facility. Department of Corrections and Rehabilitation, Stockton, CACGL Functional and Architectural Programming and Site Master Planning / HDR Design.
- David L. Moss Justice Center Mental Health Expansion, Tulsa County Dewberry Architects (López et al., 2017).

Conclusion

"As they stand today, correctional facilities are obsolete. But right now, they are often the only tool for dealing with the mentally ill coming into contact with the criminal justice system. The building solutions that are emerging to

deal with the mentally ill in corrections will not resemble jails and prisons as we know them."

- Ken Ricci, FAIA Principal Architect

The number and acuity level of prisoners with mental illnesses in prison settings continues to increase, and the institutional climate of prisons, which is harsh, is the antithesis of a therapeutic environment leading many inmates with mental illness to decompensate instead of recover. The correctional facilities have what it takes to play a major role in achieving a therapeutic mission when the physical environment is properly designed, with features that promote mental health, healing, and recovery. This includes environments that provide calming and uplifting colors and materials, natural light, clear sightlines for proactive supervision, views of the outside, open and orderly sequence of spaces, normative furnishings, and good acoustical treatment. This kind of setting needs to be comfortable, safe and should emphasize personal empowerment and promote individual dignity (López et al., 2017).

CHAPTER 11:
Mental Health Professionals and Their Role

According to officials in Nebraska prisons, the institution is currently employing an insufficient number of mental health staff hired to treat inmates. The prison is having similar problems with hiring and retaining front-line security workers along with the mental health staff. Some of the factors responsible for the shortage in the number of mental health staff are the same factors responsible for the high turnover and shortage of corrections officers, such as difficult working conditions and low wages. Of the 23 hiring slots for psychologists, the Corrections Department has only filled 11, and records show that two of the department's top psychiatrists left in more recent months, prior to the release of the report (Hammel, 2016).

There was also the retirement of the medical director, whose departure left a gap that an official termed "lack of consistent leadership." At the time of publication of this report, 35 jobs in behavioral health were unfilled. According to Dr. Alice Mitwaruciu (the acting behavior health administrator for the department), most of the clinicians that left accepted employment elsewhere; they work in less stressful environments, have fewer challenging clients, and receive better wages. According to Dr. Randy Kohl, the recently retired head of medical services for Corrections, part of the problem also stems from the fact that there is a national shortage of nurses and psychologists, which trickles down into the prison system as well (Hammel, 2016).

The components of minimally adequate mental health systems within prisons include:

- The treatment that goes beyond segregating the mentally ill inmate and increasing correctional supervision
- A systematic screening, as well as evaluation program, which will identify inmates who need mental health treatment
- The treatment by trained mental health professionals in the appropriate numbers, in order to identify as well as treat prisoners suffering from serious mental disorders
- The maintenance of complete, accurate, and confidential records of mental health treatment processes
- The proper use of psychotropic medication (prescription as well as monitoring by appropriately trained and licensed staff to treat mental disorders, rather than using them solely as a means of behavioral management, and
- A suicide prevention program (Ruiz v. Estelle)

The Importance of Health Professionals in Corrections

The management as well as care of mental health patients requires the significant contribution of several persons in order to be successful in the correctional settings, and requires they look at "psychiatrists, nursing staff, correctional officers, social workers and psychologists" and their important roles (Temporini, 2010). The starting point is the interaction between inmates and psychologists during their psychological evaluations from the moment of entry into the correctional facility.

Additionally, social workers can actually mobilize appropriate resources to assist inmates with community reinsertion, and they can work to ensure that the progress an inmate makes while in prison does not become reversed. By utilizing social workers as the final connecting piece from the treatment inside the correctional facility to services outside the prison, a continuity is establishing that ensures that prisoners are ideally set up for success after their release. However, this is not always the case, as is revealed by the high rate of recidivism (Daifotis, 2018).

Psychiatrists and Mentally Ill Inmates

Many inmates have serious mental health issues as well as chemical dependency issues, which means that they need prompt, competent, and comprehensive psychiatric care. Although the essential duties of a psychiatrist in the correctional facility are not different from those practicing in an outpatient setting, there are nuances of working in the prison environment, which includes the need to maintain security and the presence of more common types of diagnosis (Scottsdale).

When inmates have been evaluated and are determined to need medication, they are given assurances regarding receiving that medication. It's also part of the role of psychiatrists to track inmates' symptoms, carry out "assessments of suicidality," and when necessary, they may even direct therapy sessions (Temporini, 2010). Psychiatrists prove critical to the effective mental health treatment of inmates because some inmates with mental health issues will not improve without medication. Social workers also operate on behalf of prisoners with people outside the correctional institution. After an inmate is released, he or she can work with social workers to connect "with outside agencies" to continue their mental health care (Temporini, 2010).

So, What's Expected of a Prison Psychiatrist?

When practicing clinically, a prison psychiatrist has to keep up with the latest trends in research. Data in the correctional setting are interpreted based on how "typical" criminals respond, but the data are compared to a non-offender population. Correctional psychiatrists study and carry out research in areas such as malingering in prison populations, mental health disorders, dual diagnosis of substance abuse, and how to work with resistant patients (Scottsdale).

Treatment of Mentally Ill Inmates

A prison psychiatrist treats patients for major mental illnesses that respond to medication, like impulse control disorder. There are also other, secondary problems which cannot be treated with medications, such as personality disorders, including antisocial personality disorder and psychopathic personality disorder. Prison psychiatrists who are faced with an offender with this kind of dual diagnosis need to be on their guard, because a dual diagnosis inmate is likely to behave in ways that may sabotage his treatment, like pretending to take his medication while instead really selling them for profit (Scottsdale).

Maintenance of Security While Working in Prisons

For the psychiatrists, working in correctional institutions exposes them to dangerous and sometimes violent inmates. Although an episode of individual or group violence is rare in prisons, when it does occur, prison psychiatrists are specifically vulnerable because they are locked up "behind the walls," like the inmates, and often lack physical training to handle such situations. It's imperative for prison officials to always be safety-conscious while working in prisons. For instance, it's dangerous to give an inmate a pencil, to allow an inmate to make a phone call, or to give an inmate a stick of chewing gum. All these devices may actually be used against the psychiatrist as weapons or they will be stored for later use (Scottsdale).

Educating Inmates

Similar to the treatments that are obtained in a non-prison environment, a prison psychiatrist teaches patients about their mental health issues and explains the risks and benefits of treatment clearly enough for the patient to understand. The psychiatrist acts as the head of a multidisciplinary team that is responsible for constantly educating other non-mental health-oriented staff, including medical hospital workers and correctional officers, about working with offenders. Most of the teaching done by prison psychiatrists are informal and casual in nature (Scottsdale).

Roles of Psychologists in Prisons

Due to the higher proportion of inmates with mental illness in the correctional facilities, psychologists have been playing an increasing role in serving mentally ill inmates. However, as a result of the nontraditional work environment, a majority of psychologists require further motivation, such as higher pay or other incentives to encourage them to work in such an environment. If an inmate has a mental illness, he or she is usually referred for "crisis, individual, and group psychotherapy" offered by psychologists (Temporini, 2010).

The amount of therapy as well as the manner in which it's delivered are dependent on the correctional institution. Therapy is often delivered on an either individual basis or a group setting. The role of a psychologist in correctional institutions include:

- **Behavior Modification and Support-** Essentially, psychologists work as part of a team and collaborate with attorneys, caseworkers, and correctional officers to modify inmates' behavior. Throughout the entire process, the psychologist will also work with other prison staff to provide the safest environment possible for all inmates in the prison.

- **Interview and Observe New Clients-** The correctional psychologist will also interview and observe the inmate's behavior. They could ask the inmate to complete a survey or test just to assist in compiling a personality profile of the subject. The interview process may be extended to family members of the inmate, and after the initial information is obtained, the correctional psychologist will study and analyze the findings.

- **Diagnose and Treat Inmates-** The correctional psychologist is expected to use his professional training to identify clinical disorders and come up with a diagnosis. This is followed by creating the proper treatment plan and it is often done in conjunction with a group of professionals such as caseworkers, medical doctors and other professionals.

- **Integration-** While the correctional psychologist is involved from the initial introduction of an inmate down to their eventual discharge, the main objective of the psychologist is to help integrate the inmate back into society. When appropriate, the psychologist will also work with the client, their family, and their friends as a group in order to achieve treatment goals (Vicki).

In the United States, psychiatric illnesses are over-represented in prison populations compared to the general population, and, in fact, more than half of all inmates have some form of mental health diagnosis (James et al., 2006). Since correctional facilities are obligated to handle the medical and mental health needs of inmates, more psychiatrists are now practicing in jails and prisons.

Despite the increasing number of psychiatrists working in prisons across the United States, many of them had little or no education, training, or orientation regarding these specific settings. Forensic psychiatry fellowship requirements include experience in treating acutely ill as well as chronically ill inmates (ACGME).

Although correctional experience isn't precluded in general psychiatric training, it's also not required. The forensic component of general psychiatric residency is limited to report writing, the evaluation of forensic issues, and testimonies (American Psychiatric Association, 2000). Even though the work of psychiatrists in correctional settings has generally been reserved for consultation and medication management, clinicians must understand and appreciate the wider landscape and environment where they practice (Burns, 2011).

The Roles of a Correctional Nurse

As soon as an inmate starts receiving treatment, they will encounter nursing staff as well as psychiatrists. Part of the major roles of these health care professionals is the distribution of medications as well as to ensure that prisoners take the medication and do not "check" it for the purpose of either passing it to other inmates or saving it for later use (Temporini, 2010). The correctional nurse performs several tasks that are crucial to the successful treatment of inmates in correctional facilities:

1. Primary Care

Usually, correctional nurses are the first point of contact for imprisoned patients who have healthcare needs. They seek to provide all other aspects of healthcare and make determinations regarding the proper level and type of care needed. This helps them coordinate ambulatory care provision to the patient population in correctional facilities.

2. Health Promotion

The inmate patient population is usually underserved with limited healthcare access within the community. So, inmates enter the correctional system having made several poor lifestyle choices and usually have little knowledge of how they can manage chronic conditions. Therefore, it's the major role of correctional nurses to promote healthy lifestyle choices while educating the patient population at every encounter within the prison.

3. Emergency Care

They are responsible for providing immediate treatment of acute illness and injury while ascertaining if a life-threatening injury exists, which would require emergency transport to an emergency room. With the provision of first aid and basic life support, patients in need of such care are stabilized for transport.

4. Inmate Care Coordination

Correctional nurses help coordinate patient care within a system for other purposes. Several barriers to providing care must be overcome. Also, standard security constraints like restricted movement or limited personal items can inhibit continuity of care. Therefore, correctional nurses need to creatively navigate the system in order to coordinate appropriate care for each individual inmate based on their needs (Schoenly).

Challenges Psychiatrists Face in Correctional Institutions

The psychiatrist is often regarded as a guest in the correctional institution, but that's not entirely accurate. The US constitution guaranteed access to health care, and this includes mental health treatment. However, the parameters of care delivery, most times, becomes affected to a great extent by the needs as well as priorities of correctional facility, and the first priority of all correctional institutions is security. The successful correctional psychiatrist as earlier mentioned must learn to work with correctional officers and always has to keep safety in mind (Simpson, 2014).

These safety concerns may override the psychiatrist's priorities, especially when it comes to issues like the timing of appointments, patient housing assignments, or whether a specific patient can be seen face-to-face or at the cell door. Additionally, a psychiatrist may not be able to see a patient during "lockdown." While there is a collaboration between the psychiatrist and correctional officers, the psychiatrist doesn't have the final say regarding certain various issues (Simpson, 2014).

The limitations on the confidentiality witnessed in a non-correctional setting is another challenge psychiatrists face. It's a common practice in a jail setting for custody personnel to retain direct visual contact during clinical interview for safety reasons, especially when the inmate is exhibiting disorganized behavior, becomes hostile, or is agitated. If an interview needs to be conducted at the cell door, then cell mates as well as other inmates near the client may likely hear some of the things discussed. Although the correctional psychiatrists may try to take all feasible steps to protect confidentiality, it's often not possible (Simpson, 2014).

Due to the high rates of substance abuse disorders among inmates, the misuse of medications is another common problem that psychiatrists encounter. The prescription of stimulant medications for the treatment of ADHD has actually been banned by some correctional facilities as a result of their obvious abuse potential, while others permit their use under tight control (Appelbaum, 2009).

Also, a number of other stimulants and benzodiazepines, as well as some other psychiatric medications, are often sought after and bartered for nonmedical use like bupropion and quetiapine. In fact, bupropion can be crushed and snorted by inmates to receive a stimulant-like effect and quetiapine is usually desired as a soporific (Tamburello et al., 2012; Hilliard et al., 2013).

However, despite the various challenges of correctional psychiatry, it can also be highly rewarding. Many mentally ill inmates have very complex histories and comorbidities which might often include a history of foster care placement, childhood trauma, long-term poverty, substance abuse, homelessness, traumatic brain injury and several other medical problems that are related to substance abuse and/or lack of regular medical care. Psychiatrists can gain satisfaction from the intellectual challenge of evaluating and treating such patients (Simpson, 2014).

It is also an opportunity to make a positive difference for socially marginalized and severely ill inmates who have been unable or unwilling to access care in the community and to change their condition. There is a need for significant adjustments while effectively practicing psychiatry in the correctional setting. Although some correctional psychiatrists gain experience via elective rotations during residency or required placements during forensic psychiatry fellowship, a majority of them learn the peculiar features of the correctional environment while "on the job." While the psychiatrist understands the challenges and has learned to navigate them, working with inmates with mental illness can provide an opportunity to help some of the most disadvantaged members of society and can prove to be an interesting professional challenge (Simpson, 2014).

CHAPTER 12:
Transitional Challenges & Recidivism

In the United States, about 600,000 men and women are released from various correctional facilities each year (Harrison et al., 2003). However, professionals are now becoming more aware of the high risk of recidivism with inmates who are not given support services which help them integrate successfully into society. The absence of effective and efficient mental health treatment (including the appropriate support for employment, housing, and income) likely contributes significantly to the number of mentally ill inmates who commit and recommit various criminal offenses. They end up cycling in and out of prison facilities for several years. When looking at the estimates on recidivism rates, several studies indicate that mentally ill offenders have higher rates of recidivism (Human Rights Watch, 2003).

For instance, a 2005 study estimated that over 75 percent of mentally ill inmates had been arrested previously. Recently, in 2017, an additional study revealed that mentally ill inmates have a nine percent chance of being rearrested one year after their release. The difference increases to 15 percent after five years of their release. Also, the same study discovered that inmates with severe mental illness are four percent more likely to be arrested again than those with milder conditions (Sahlin, 2018).

The Correlation between Mental Illness and Recidivism

It is important to clarify that some studies on the relationship between inmate mental illness and recidivism have been characterized as being contradictory and inconclusive. Some of the shortcomings of these studies include their methodology, namely, the use of single definitions of recidivism, making use of small sample sizes, limited post-release follow-up periods on the timing of recidivism and lack of sufficient control variables (Bales et al., 2017).

However, a 2017 study attempted to address these fundamental, methodological deficiencies that were identified in previous literature on inmate mental illness and recidivism (Bales et al., 2017). The study was able to overcome the shortcoming of the previous studies by employing multiple measures of recidivism and also extending post-release follow-up from one and two years to three, four, and five years, while utilizing a large cohort of 200,889 inmates and also applying a much more comprehensive set of control variables that have been identified to be associated with recidivism (Bales et al., 2017).

The conclusion of these research findings can be seen below:

- The first research question aimed to find out if a mental health diagnosis had a positive, negative, or a null effect on the chances of post-prison recidivating. The study discovered that there was a remarkable, positive association between any mental health diagnosis, and specifically, a serious mental health diagnosis, in connection with the likelihood of recidivating after release. Additionally, when the models were broken down by year using the logistic regression models, a majority of the associations between recidivism measures and mental health diagnoses were remarkably positive. However, research findings indicate that serious mental health diagnoses only had a meaningful, positive association with the first two follow-up years on rearrests and had a negative association with the final follow-up year on re-conviction. As such, the overall answer to the first question is that a mental illness diagnosis has a positive effect upon post-release recidivism.

- The second research question was: does a mental health diagnosis have a differential effect on different measures of recidivism, mainly in terms of re-arrest, reconviction, and re-incarceration? The survival analysis discovered similar effects across all three recidivism outcomes for the two independent variables, any mental health diagnosis as well as serious mental health diagnosis. The results indicate that a diagnosis of serious mental illness was only significant with regards to re-arrest and re-conviction.

- The third research question sought to find out whether a mental health diagnosis differentially affects time it takes an inmate to recidivate. Based on the positive association that was found in all survival analysis models, there are indications that both the presence of any mental illness, and especially a serious mental illness, increased the chances that an offender would recidivate after being released.

- The fourth question seeks to answer whether inmates with serious mental illness (namely, Major Depressive Disorder, Psychotic Disorders, and Schizophrenia) are more, less or no more likely to recidivate than those with a less serious mental illness. The results of the study indicated that both survival models, as well as the logistic regression models, show that people diagnosed with a severe mental health illness (rather than any mental health diagnosis) were not only more likely to recidivate, but likely to recidivate even sooner (Bales et al., 2017).

The Cycle of Incarceration for Mentally Ill Inmates

Although current correctional facilities treat inmates more humanely than how they have in the past, offenders having mental illnesses still have other struggles to deal with as well, such as discrimination. A person with a severe mental illness (as mentioned earlier in previous chapters) is likely to get a longer, as well as harsher sentence than a neurotypical peer who was convicted of the same crime. Also, such inmates are less likely to be granted release. Incarceration can worsen mental health; strict rules, as well as isolation, can increase stress in an inmate. Also, an individual may experience additional mental health issues as they adjust to the transition (Sahlin, 2018).

For instance, the Bureau of Justice Statistics carried out a survey and asked inmates about their mental health within the last 30 days. The response revealed that 14 percent of federal and state inmates disclosed having severe psychological distress, a rate which was almost doubled for jail inmates, putting them at 26 percent. The American incarceration system functions as a perfect recipe to perpetuate habitual patterns for people (Sahlin, 2018).

People become demoralized because of extreme isolation and societal alienation, to the extent that the only form of self-regulation becomes substances. This is one of the ways that drug addiction and alcohol spreads through correctional facilities. According to Trey Cole, PsyD, "Relationally speaking, incarcerated individuals often become accustomed to the externally controlled environment (i.e., when to eat, sleep, etc.). When released, then, usually with few resources, becoming accountable to oneself and internally motivated become more difficult.

Inmates who have been released may be without support or resources. They might have issues getting employment or housing because of stigma surrounding their label as an ex-convict. Also, reduced mental health can make it harder for someone to make a living. Thus, the same factors that led an individual to criminal activities in the first place may actually be stronger after their release. Their ability to fend for themselves and survive within the law may be reduced, and in this context, an individual can easily be drawn to recidivism (Sahlin, 2018).

When there is no discharge plan or transitional services, mentally ill parolees are more likely to decompensate, violate the conditions of release, commit new offenses, and return to prison (Council of State Governments, 2002). If post-release services are to be effective, they should be intensive and ongoing. According to a report by Lovell, Gagliardi, and Peterson (2002), 73 percent of mentally ill inmates who were released from Washington State correctional facilities received social or mental health services. However, few of them received clinically meaningful levels of care in their first year of release and a majority of them (70 percent) were rearrested for new charges or parole violations. Additionally, the study mentioned that those who committed more serious crimes received fewer services and also received services later than those who committed less serious crimes.

Various studies have indicated that court-mandated drug treatment, making use of the leverage of the court, as well as the criminal justice systems leads to an increase in enrollment and participation in interventions and programs and also lowers criminal activity (Lurigio, 2002). Additionally, these findings might actually apply to the effects of involuntary or coerced mental health treatment (Colvin et al., 2002).

It has been revealed by research that involuntary treatment for mentally ill offenders (MIOs) can dramatically increase their compliance with medication and remarkably lower their chances of psychiatric and criminal recidivism (Heilbrum et al., 1993 & Lamb et al., 1999). It has also been revealed that coercion is most effective in reducing recidivism among mentally ill inmates when it's properly balanced with supportive services (Draine, 2003).

Lowering Recidivism Rates

According to a report by the Council of State Governments (CSG) Justice Center, the way the US criminal justice systems handle individuals with mental health issues needs to be redesigned and overhauled. They called for special attention to be paid to mentally ill inmates who are released from correctional facilities. The CSG recommended that a successful system of reentry into society has to meet the following criteria:

1. Combine various services and professional efforts.
2. Properly coordinate treatment for substance abuse as well as other mental health problems.
3. Integrate primary health care and mental health care.
4. Provide housing for former inmates with mental health issues.
5. Take advantage of family connections and community resources for treatment.
6. Make sure that individuals who are released from the correctional facility can access the full range of government entitlements that they are eligible for, like Disability Insurance and Social Security (Sahlin, 2018).

Some states have already commenced with the implementation of these measures. States including Texas, Colorado and North Carolina have used grant money to expand mental health care services as well as substance abuse treatment for offenders. This has also yielded tremendous results for them, for instance:

- Texas recorded a 25 percent reduction in the 3-year re-incarceration rate between 2004 and 2013.
- North Carolina also had a reduction of 42 percent in individuals who were sent back to prison after probation violations between 2006 and 2015.
- Colorado witnessed probation revocations and saw the 3-year re-incarceration rate lowered by at least 23 percent within the same time frame (Sahlin, 2018).

Reducing Recidivism through Diversion

Diversion tactics have given indications of a reduction in the rate of recidivism for individuals with mental illness. Diversion has to do with the practice of placing inmates in mental health treatment rather than keeping them in correctional facilities. Generally, it takes one or two forms. Forensic hospitalization is the first form, and in these cases, inmates that have been found not guilty as a result of insanity are usually sent to forensic hospitals (Sahlin, 2018).

Hospitals of this type confine people just like jails and prisons do, but their aim is mainly rehabilitation rather than punishment. In the criminal justice system, less than 1 percent of people qualify for the insanity defense. According to a study that was released in 2005, inmates that were released from forensic hospitals had very low rates of recidivism. In addition, they were less likely to re-offend than offenders having mental health problems, and less likely to offend than offenders without a diagnosis (Sahlin, 2018).

The second form of diversion has to do with mental health courts. Mental health courts are mainly for inmates with mental illness but do not qualify for the insanity defense. Judges may offer defendants reduced sentences in exchange for treatment. In several cases, a defendant may not be jailed or imprisoned at all (Sahlin, 2018).

According to a 2007 study, participation in mental health courts lowered the risk of committing a violent offense in half. Individuals who have gone through mental health courts also stayed longer in society without reoffending than others that passed through the traditional courts. The National Alliance on Mental Health (NAMI) is a strong supporter of diversion as an approach that is more humane and cost-effective. According to NAMI, the cost of incarcerating adults with a mental illness is two to three times higher than the cost of maintaining other offenders. Thus, it's often cheaper to send nonviolent inmates to receive mental health treatment rather than jail. Prioritizing treatment over punishment could offer lasting benefits for the criminal justice system (Sahlin, 2018).

The result of the study on the positive relationship between inmate mental illness diagnoses and recidivism has resulted in a number of research and policy implications about the potential and the value of in-prison and reentry mental health programs and services. Mental illnesses among prisoners increases their chances to recidivate (Bales et al., 2017).

Consequently, in-prison and community mental health systems need to be sufficient in capacity and also coordinated and integrated. Although mental health in-prison programs and services are required, they have to be aligned and coordinated with community mental health services that provide inmates' releases with a mental health continuum of care based on best practices for successful reentry. The collaboration between the community health service providers as well as correctional professionals is crucial with information-sharing protocols and the use of recognized standards for in-prison and community mental health practices (Bales et al., 2017).

CHAPTER 13:
Juvenile Mental Illness and Treatment

"Sixty-five to seventy percent of children in the juvenile justice system have a diagnosable mental health condition, and children in the juvenile justice system have substantially higher rates of behavioral health conditions than children in the general population. At least seventy-five percent of youth in the juvenile justice system experienced traumatic victimization, and ninety-three percent reported exposure to adverse childhood experiences including child abuse, family and community violence, and serious illness."

— *(Baglivio et al., 2014)*

The reliance on the juvenile justice system to meet the needs of juvenile offenders having mental health issues has greatly increased over the past decade. The juvenile justice system is currently faced with the task of not only providing proper mental assessments of youths but also providing effective treatment services for those individuals. Originally, the juvenile justice system was both a rehabilitative and preventive approach which emphasized the various needs and rights of children over the appeal to punish them (Garascia, 2005; Statistics Canada, 2004; Sickmund, 2004).

The incarceration of a sizeable proportion of these children and adolescents is as a result of violent, aggressive and antisocial behaviors. There is evidence to suggest that aggression and violence are not actually the only problems that youths face and perhaps they may not even be the most serious. Based on research, there is growing evidence that the majority of youths and children within correctional settings suffer from one or more mental disorders (Abram, Teplin, McClelland & Dulcan, 2003; Andre, Pease, Kendall & Boulton, 1994; Uzlen & Hamilton, 1998).

Presently, urgent calls are being made to respond to the treatment and rehabilitation needs of children and adolescents within these settings because the mental health prognosis for many of them is poor. The general consensus across studies indicates that a majority of incarcerated youths actually meet the criteria for at least one DSMIV disorder and about 20 percent of youths further meet the diagnostic criteria for serious mental disorders — a serious emotional disturbance leading to functional impairment (Cocozza & Skowyra, 2000).

History of Juvenile Mental Illness

As observed by Garascia (2005), originally, the juvenile justice system was both rehabilitative and also preventative in approach, which emphasized the needs and rights of youths over the appeal to punish them. Based on the Juvenile Justice and Delinquency Prevention Act of 1974, the major goal of juvenile justice was to separate the youth from the formal punitive processing of the adult justice system, and this led to the use of community-based programs instead of larger institutions. There was, however, an interesting shift in the treatment of juvenile offenders in the justice system in the 1980s and 1990s. Before the 1980s, juvenile offenders were seen as rehabilitative but due to a surge in violent delinquency, this perspective was short-lived, and the protection of the community became the main goal (Underwood et al., 2016).

Consequently, a new approach was developed by the juvenile justice system which favors the punishment/criminalization perspective over a rehabilitative/medicalization perspective. Also, just like the zero-tolerance attitude of the education system during the early 1990s, over half of the states in the United States made revisions that enabled juvenile offenders to be prosecuted easily in the adult criminal court, and this was followed by punitive laws passed to address adolescent crime (Fried et al., 2001; Wald et al., 2003).

Although there was a shift in the US justice system from a punitive approach to a rehabilitative model of care, it was not focused on community-based provision of services but on youth corrections systems to care for the mental health and other specialized needs of juvenile offenders. As a result of this development, many juvenile justice systems were ill-equipped to properly deal with the acute needs of juveniles with mental health disorders. The United States Department of Justice (USDJ) has several investigations providing evidence that mental health services for youth in juvenile justice is usually inadequate or entirely unavailable (USDJ, 2011). Some of the barriers that counter the provision of adequate services include:

- Inadequate administrative capacity
- Insufficient policy development
- Lack of training for staff
- Insufficient resources
- Lack of appropriate staffing

Juvenile corrections personnel are seriously hindered from providing adequate services to youth offenders having mental health concerns due to factors such as lack of research, insufficient policy development, inadequate models of care, inadequate practice and ineffective experience and training of staff.

Juvenile Mental Illness in the Justice System

The population of youth having mental disorders within the juvenile justice system has been found to be consistently higher than within the general population of adolescents. Based on estimates, approximately 50-70 percent of about 2 million youth involved in the juvenile justice system meet the criteria for mental health disorders. Also, approximately 40-80 percent of incarcerated juveniles have been identified to have at least one diagnosable mental health disorder. In previous studies of juvenile offender detention facilities, two-thirds of males and three-quarters of females were found to meet the criteria for at least a mental health disorder while one-third met the criteria for substance use disorder (Underwood et al., 2016).

Several comprehensive studies have revealed that certain types of mental illness are common among juvenile offenders and some symptoms actually increase the risk of youth engaging in aggressive behaviors. It is also important to note that the risk of aggression increases for many specific disorders and comorbid disorders due to the fact that the emotional symptoms such as anger and self-regulatory symptoms tend to increase such risk (Stoddard-Dare et al., 2011; Teplin et al., 2002; Wasserman et al., 2002; and Atkins et al., 1999).

Some common mental disorders found in youth offenders include:

- Affective disorders such as:
- Persistent depression
- Manic episodes; and
- Major depression
- Anxiety disorders such as:

  o Panic, generalized anxiety

  o Post-traumatic stress disorder

  o Obsessive-compulsive disorder

- Psychotic disorders
- Disruptive behavior disorders such as:

  o Attention deficit hyperactivity disorder, and

  o Conduct oppositional defiant disorder

- Substance use disorders (Underwood et al., 2016).

According to some sources, understanding the link between youth offending and mental health difficulties is crucial when considering the treatment response because there is sufficient evidence to suggest that mental health difficulties are linked directly and indirectly to later offending behavior by youths (Heilbrum et al., 2005).

Mood disorders, especially depression, occur in 10-25 percent of youths in the juvenile justice system and the irritable mood that is usually associated with depressive disorders increases youths' chances of inciting angry responses from other people, which will increase their risk of engaging in acts which are physically aggressive causing them to get arrested (Grisso, 2008: Loeber et al., 1994; and Takeda, 2000).

However, the mood disorder of the adolescent may increase the risk of altercations with others while in custody or even increase the risk of anger at oneself leading to self-injurious behaviors. The high prevalence of juvenile mental disorders within the juvenile justice system does not actually require the need for treatment, but rather, it emphasizes the urgent need for different levels of mental health care with various treatment options provided.

While some youths that meet the criteria for a disorder experience these disorders only temporarily and only require emergency services, others with chronic mental health needs will likely require clinical care well into adulthood. Although some juvenile offenders will function well despite their symptoms, others may show limited functionality. There is a need, therefore, for effective screening and assessment processes to help deal with different individual needs and also provide varied effective treatment options. There is no doubt such tasks are weighty for just one system to handle effectively (Roberts et al., 1998).

Juvenile Mental Illness and Effective Treatment

There are several supporting pieces of evidence to show that it's beneficial to treat youth in acute distress as a result of mental illness. Many types of psychosocial and psychotherapeutic interventions are available for juveniles with mental disorders which focus mainly on youth having mental health difficulties and delinquent behaviors. Although there is limited evidence to confirm the efficacy of some of these approaches, some effective therapeutic models having promising evidence for their effectiveness in treating youth offenders are available and some of them will be treated below.

Functional Family Therapy (FFT)

This approach is a brief family-centered approach that was developed in the 1960s. It was developed in response to multi-need youth and families and is used for youths between the ages of 11 to 18 who are at risk for and/or presenting with delinquency, conduct disorder, violence, disruptive behavior disorders, substance abuse, and oppositional defiant disorder. Based on reports from the National Mental Health Association, a five-year follow-up study discovered that less than 10 percent of juveniles receiving Functional Family Therapy, versus 60 percent of youth found in juvenile court, had records for subsequent arrests. According to research, while FFT has proved to be an effective model for reducing recidivism, the training of behavioral health providers in the FFT model is essential (Shelton, 2005).

The Multisystemic Therapy

The multisystemic therapy is one of the best available treatment approaches for juvenile offenders having mental health needs as indicated by empirical literature. It is an intensive multi-modal family-based approach that is suitable for treating identified causal factors and also correlating factors of delinquency and substance abuse. It is effective for treating juvenile offenders with emotional and behavioral problems. As demonstrated by studies, it has led to reductions as high as 70 percent in the rates of re-arrest, improvements in familial functioning, reductions of up to 64 percent in out-of-home placements, as well as decreases in the mental health concerns for serious youth offenders (National Mental Health Association, 2004).

Multidimensional Treatment Foster Care (MTFC)

It is an alternative to residential, secure-care, group or hospitalization treatment process for adolescents having severe and chronic emotional and behavioral disorders. This type of care allows adolescents to be placed with trained local and supervised families for about 6-9 months. During the MTFC placement, family therapy is carried out.

The National Mental Health Association research about the program has indicated that youth juvenile offenders spent 60 percent fewer days incarcerated than those that did not receive the services and they also had significantly fewer arrests. The treatment approach was found to decelerate girl's depressive symptoms and provided greater benefits for girls having higher levels of initial depressive symptoms (Leve et al., 2007; Harold et al., 2013).

Diversion

The Mental Health America organization is of the view that most youths do not need to be incarcerated, rather, as much as is possible, the children should be diverted away from the juvenile justice system toward community-based services and behavioral health treatment where needed, especially for technical probation violations and non-violent offenses. The treatment of children having behavioral health conditions is most effective when properly planned and integrated at the local level with other effective services provided by community organizations, child welfare agencies, and schools (Mental Health America, 2015).

The services need to be strength-based, recovery-oriented, family-focused, trauma-informed, individualized, and suitable for the child's gender, age, culture, and language. The main thrust of diversion is that youths should be positively engaged and also integrated in their communities and families. Generally, when it comes to diversion, youths require the following:

- The chance to foster and nurture connections,
- The opportunity to explore, discuss, and also reflect on their ideas,
- The opportunity to create a lasting impact within their community,
- The chance to embrace creativity,
- A chance to be mentored on how to make good life decisions, and

- Access to have emotional safety (Mental Health America, 2015).

The Blueprint for Change

The following key principles actually form the basis for the National Center for Mental Health and Juvenile Justice's (NCMHJJ) blueprint for change (A comprehensive Model for the Identification and Treatment of Youth with Mental Health Needs in Contact with the Juvenile Justice System:

- Young persons should not have to enter the juvenile justice system in order to have access to mental health services.
- When possible, juveniles with mental health conditions should be diverted to receive evidence-based mental health treatment in community settings.
- The information that is collected to help provide mental health screening should not be used to jeopardize the legal interests of children as defendants.
- In the event that it is impossible to divert youth out of the justice system, they should be placed in the least restrictive environment that also has access to evidence-based treatment.
- The mental health services should be consistent with the developmental realities of youth.
- The mental health services that are provided for the children should respond to issues such as ethnicity, gender, sexual orientation, race, socio-economic status, age, and religion.
- There must be a regular evaluation of the services and strategies for serving children in the juvenile justice system in order to determine their effectiveness.
- Planning and services for children has to be based on close collaboration among education, juvenile justice, and other systems.
- Mental health services need to be consistent with the developmental realities of children (Skowyra et al., 2007).

Juvenile Competency

The mental health assessment of youth offenders assists in determining how the system can help to address their treatment needs. It helps to address the legal issues regarding a juvenile's competency to understand the adjudicatory process and participate in it thoughtfully and make decisions as part of the process. Ideally, incompetence to stand trial has to do with a mental disorder or developmental disability. Juvenile competency is greatly complicated by developmental immaturity with limited guidance in law regarding how to deal with it. Developmental immaturity is a factor that distinguishes many juveniles from adults in very crucial ways that make them less qualified to assist in their defense or even make important decisions as part of the process. Generally, juveniles have the rights afforded to adult defendants, which includes the right to be competent to stand trial and a right to counsel (Hammond, 2007).

Conclusion

Each year, an estimated 2 million youths that are under the age of 18 are arrested in the United States which translates to about 5,000 delinquency cases each day. Although, approximately 95 percent of those arrested are accused of non-violent crimes such as rape, murder and aggravated assault, they are still incarcerated in the juvenile justice system. This leads to more harm to the social, academic and personal growth of the youth despite the efforts made to reduce incarceration. A large number of youths in the juvenile justice system have diagnosable mental health disorder and about 75 percent of youth in the juvenile justice system have also experienced traumatic victimization like domestic abuse, physical abuse and traumatic neglect which made them vulnerable to health disorders and PTSD (Fisher, 2015). Correctional facilities have a duty to provide adequate medical services which includes treatment services for mental health and substance abuse, and they are to ensure the protection of youths from harm.

Conclusion

"Correctional facilities may be places that provide structure... but jails and prisons should not be perceived of as places of sanctuary because they do not operate according to a therapeutic orientation and do not necessarily provide relief to persons in distress."

(Knoll, 2006)

The US makes up just 5 percent of the world's population, and yet has 25 percent of the world's prison population, with a total of 2.2 million people that are confined in various jails and prisons across the United States. There has been a steady increase in the number of incarcerated individuals having psychiatric or psychological disorders since the 1960s, and this was as a result of the deinstitutionalization of the state mental health system. Based on a study by the Urban Institute in March 2015, an estimate of 56 percent of state inmates, 45 percent of federal prisoners and 64 percent of jail inmates suffer from one or more psychological disorders (Pittaro, 2015).

Also, in 2014, the American Psychiatric Association reported that a majority of the common mental illnesses suffered by inmates include schizophrenia, depression and bipolar disorder. Correctional facilities have become the *de facto* state hospitals that are responsible for the confinement and care of the mentally ill persons. Presently, the correctional institutions accommodate more mentally ill inmates than other US hospitals combined. This implies that there is a need for a paradigm shift both in thinking, policy, and practice (Pittaro, 2015).

Clearly, the correctional institutions were not meant to handle the extreme influx of people having several levels of mental illness. Although the health conditions of mentally ill inmates are not necessarily correlated with criminality, the intensity, as well as the frequency of these disorders, are quite higher within most prisons in the United States. This suggests that the disorders may at least contribute indirectly to criminality. The provision of mental health, substance abuse and medical treatment for these mentally ill inmates is often challenging especially when considering the fact that most correctional facilities are not adequately equipped to deal with those mental illnesses adequately (Pittaro, 2015).

So, how should corrections professionals respond to this issue that has persisted for so long?

First, it's important to note that some of the moves by the government to address the issue of mental illness in correctional facilities have been slow and challenging, but worth mentioning. For instance, the police departments are in partnership with health departments and social services in communities to establish pre-arrest and pre-booking diversion programs (Houston Behavioral Healthcare Hospital, 2016).

Another effort is the establishment of a Crisis Intervention Team in over 2,700 communities to help train law enforcement and health providers, as well as the affected persons, in the proper response to severe cases involving mental illness, the community resources that are available as well as the process of involuntary hospitalization. The main goal of all these programs is the diversion of mentally ill persons to community-based assistance instead of arresting them (Houston Behavioral Healthcare Hospital, 2016).

It is crucial for the United States to maintain an effective and efficient public mental health treatment system which will help to lower the number of individuals with mental illness that end up in correctional facilities. Several recommendations have been made by the Treatment Advocacy Center Study:

1. All outdated and inadequate mental illness treatment laws and practices in the community should be reformed to eliminate the barriers to treatment for people that are too ill to realize

that they need care. This ensures that they get help before they become so disordered to the point of committing acts leading to their arrest, prosecution, and subsequent incarceration.

2. Prison and jail laws should be reformed to enable inmates with mental illnesses to receive appropriate and necessary treatment just as inmates with other medical conditions do.

3. Implement and promote additional programs, like mental health courts.

4. Make use of court-ordered outpatient treatment to provide the support needed by at-risk individuals to live safely and successfully within the community.

5. Encourage the comprehensive cost studies that will compare the actual cost of housing people with serious mental illness in correctional facilities and jails to the cost of adequately treating them in the community.

6. Create a careful inmate intake screening that will help to identify the medication needs of inmates, suicidal thoughts and ideations, self-destructive behaviors, anger outbursts, and other risks that are associated with mental illness.

7. Institute a mandatory release planning to ensure community support and foster recovery (Pittaro, 2015).

These recommendations are made based on the general premise that individuals with mental illness would be served better in hospitals rather than correctional facilities. But the public mental illness treatment system is not in good shape and also requires desperate repair, which can only come from widespread reform (Pittaro, 2015).

According to a three-year randomized-control study which was carried out by clinical researchers at the University of Rochester Medical Center's department of psychiatry, the Rochester Forensic Assertive Community Treatment model (R-FACT) withstood rigorous examination and has offered promising results:

> *"Our research suggests that it's possible to prevent criminal recidivism among people with even the most severe mental*

illnesses and substantial criminal histories," the study principal investigator J. Steven Lamberti, professor of psychiatry. "We found that by combining the expertise of mental health and criminal justice professionals in a certain way, we can promote both individual health and public safety."

(Roth-Rochester, 2017).

R-FACT "promotes patient engagement in treatment and community tenure through collaboration with criminal justice partners. Such efforts will likely have large beneficial downstream effects for this population," says co-investigator and forensic psychiatrist Robert L. Weisman.

According to Lamberti, individuals with severe mental illness have higher rates of criminogenic risk factors in addition to other issues that affect the way they relate to others. The key to preventing recidivism is engaging such persons in specific interventions targeting the things driving their involvement with the criminal justice system (Roth-Rochester, 2017).

Engaging individuals in treatment – especially individuals that are resistant or fearful of it – is the most challenging part. So, getting probation officers, lawyers, as well as other criminal justice professionals, involved in the program is critical. Mental health and criminal justice professionals need to problem-solve together to discover therapeutic alternatives to punishment. Our clients are men and women that feel demoralized and discouraged; they are at their very lowest point and need more rewards than sanctions (Roth-Rochester, 2017).

Summary of Terms
and Definitions

There are thousands of psychological terms used by correctional practitioners in the general institutional population settings as well as the correctional mental health settings. Below are a few terms and definitions that can help one understand the inner workings of these correctional and mental health settings.

Administrative Segregation- This is a housing unit inside the prison that is separated from the other units. The prisoners are kept in the cells all the time and are allowed to carry out outdoor activities (exercise), go for medical checkup and attend to other specific needs. Most prisoners who have violated prison rules are managed and confined in segregated housing units.

Administrative Detention- This is a kind of separation of an individual from the general community when the continued presence of an inmate may pose a threat to property, to life, to the disciplined operation of the institution, to themselves, or to staff. Administrative detention in juvenile corrections is not to last more than 24 hours, excluding holidays and weekends (Correctional Glossary of Terms).

Antisocial Personality Disorder- Individuals with antisocial personality disorder have a reckless disregard for other people, including themselves. Most individuals having antisocial personality disorder are male. An individual with this condition often finds it hard to conform to social norms and engages in behaviors that include willfully manipulating others just for personal gain, stealing, destroying properties or overindulging in pleasure-seeking behavior.

For instance, they might drive while drunk, engage in risky sex,

Mentally Ill Inmates and Corrections

speed, or use drugs. As a result of this impulsiveness, life may be a greater struggle for them. They usually move from one job to the other and have difficulty in maintaining successful relationships. In the military, they often get dishonorably discharged because of their unethical or criminal behavior. The guiltless pattern of social irresponsibility that is demonstrated by those with antisocial personality disorder starts during childhood or early adolescence (Black, 2017).

Avoidant Personality Disorder- Individuals with this kind of personality disorder suffer long-standing feelings of inadequacy. They are extremely sensitive to what other people think about them and this kind of sensitivity often causes them to be socially inhibited and feel socially inept. Due to the emotions associated with the personality disorder (feelings of inadequacy and inhibition), those with this condition often tend to avoid school, work, or other activities that would otherwise allow them to socialize or interact with people (Bressert, 2017).

Bipolar Disorder- Also known as manic-depressive illness, bipolar disorder is a brain disorder which leads to unusual shifts in energy, mood, activity levels and also the ability to execute daily tasks (National Institute of Mental Health).

Borderline Personality Disorder (BPD) - One of the main features of borderline personality disorder is the recurring and long-standing pattern of having unstable relationships with other people. This could be friendships, romantic relationships, or their relationship with family members. Also, the condition is associated with an effort to avoid feeling abandoned (whether it is real or not), and impulsivity in decision-making. Those suffering from borderline personality disorder often move easily and quickly from one emotion to the other and there is a frequent change in their self-image (Grohol, 2018).

Community Transition Program (CTP) - This is a Department of Corrections (DOC) program which helps the community transition for adult offenders and makes available a link between the community and the DOC by providing programming and case management assistance in establishing community transition plans.

Contraband- This refers to any item or items that were discovered in the correctional facility, which includes drugs that were improperly possessed (legal or illegal) and also various weapons that are prohibited by those that were legally charged with the responsibility of the operation and/or administration of the correctional facility. Basically, contrabands include but are not limited to the following:

a. Any kind of authorized item that is used for unauthorized purposes
b. Items that the institution(s) did not issue to an offender
c. Other items which an offender doesn't have the special authorization for from the Superintendent or Warden of the facility
d. Personal properties of an inmate that was not obtained through the proper means, prescribed by, or in excess of policy, and
e. Other items that pose as a risk to the order and security of an institution (Correctional Glossary of Terms).

Correctional Officer (CO) - Within federal penitentiaries, state prisons, and local jails, a correctional officer is an individual that serves as the voice of authority and also seeks to ensure the safety and welfare of inmates. They disrupt violent confrontations, assist in the rehabilitation of inmates, and maintain order within the institution (Correctionalofficeredu.org). The title, "jail guard" was used for many years to describe a correctional officer title. It is considered by most correctional professionals as a negative and disrespectful term.

Decompensation- This is the aggravation of symptoms of mental illness resulting in a significant deterioration from initial adequate levels of functioning and coping in daily life (Human Rights Watch, 2003).

Deinstitutionalization- This is the gradual transfer of inmate residents to regular community-based housing. Deinstitutionalization is accompanied by the development of services which supports inclusion and participation in the community. It also provides support, assistance that is personal and flexible, and coordination so that individuals can live the kind of lives they desire (Open Society Foundations, 2015).

Depressive Disorders- This is an illness that involves the physical human body, as well as one's mood and thoughts. Depressive disorder is a condition that interferes with normal functioning, daily life, and leads to pain for the individual with the illness and those taking care of him/her (Psychology Today).

Depression- It is known by several other names such as major depression, the blues, and biological depression. It is the feeling of sadness which can last for weeks and even months, not just a passing blue mood of one or two days. Those who are depressed often experience a lack of energy and have a sense of hopelessness, finding no pleasure in those things they previously enjoyed in the past (Grohol, 2018).

Difference between a Prison and Jail- Basically, the main difference between a jail and a prison has to do with the duration of the stay of inmates. Jails are often run by local government agencies and/or local law enforcement and they are designed to accommodate inmates that are awaiting trial or those serving a short sentence. Usually, "short" is designated as a misdemeanor conviction versus a felony, which implies that in circumstances where misdemeanor sentences are run consecutively, an individual may actually spend more than one year in jail.

Jails usually operate work release programs and boot camps, while others also offer substance abuse programs, as well as educational and vocational programs. Most of these programs are designed in a way to assist inmates to change their lives and to improve their lives in order to stand a better chance of not returning to jail. Such programs also have the added benefit of keeping the inmates occupied, which will make it less likely for them to cause problems for jailers.

On the other hand, prisons are mainly operated either by the Federal Bureau of Prisons (BOP) or state governments. They are designed to accommodate offenders that have been convicted of crimes that are more serious, typically any felony. Typically, prisons hold felons and individuals that have sentences of over one year, though the length of the sentence may vary by state.

Also, prisons offer various kinds of programs to prisoners based on the level of custody of the inmate (solitary confinement, minimum, medium or maximum security, and several others). Since prisons are designed to accommodate inmates for a long-term sentence, they are usually developed for the living needs of their population, unlike jails that have a more transient population with facilities that are less well-developed. Consequently, many inmates often prefer to stay in prisons because they will have access to more regular life, greater availability of programs, and better facilities (HG.org).

Emergency Medical Care- This includes emergency medical, mental health, or dental care for an unexpected health need or an acute illness that cannot be deferred until the next scheduled clinic or sick call.

Health Care Provider- All DOC individuals and any staff that are under contract and assigned to the DOC, and this includes the Department of Social Services as well as Department of Health staff. It also includes student interns that provide medical, dental, optometric or mental care in a DOC institution and outside specialists/referrals who provide various health care services to an offender.

Health Screening- It is a system of structured observation and inquiry designed to prevent inmates who have newly arrived and who pose a safety or health threat to other inmates, staff and themselves, from being admitted to the general population. It is also meant to help identify inmates that are in need of immediate medical attention.

High Risk of Violence Inmate- These are inmates that have been identified as level 2 or level 3 system risk through a psychopathy/violence evaluation or due to their placement in institutional disciplinary behavior, sex offender typology/evaluation/assessment, or criminal typology.

Hospitalization- A situation where an inmate is placed in a private or public medical care facility outside the institution. However, it does not include the placement of inmates in an infirmary that is operated on the grounds of the facility.

Immediate Family- An offender's legal children, spouse, biological brother (including half-brother), biological parents, step-children, biological sister (including half-sister), step sisters, step parents, step brothers, great grandparents, grandparents, sister-in-law, brother-in-law (spouse of inmate's sister or brother), father-in-law, and mother-in-law.

Inmate Health Plan- This is an individualized manual that outlines the plan for rendering medical services to inmates. It is to be developed by the DOC health care provider, approved by the DOC, and is regularly updated as needed.

Institution/Facility- It is a name given to all offices and buildings that are owned, leased operated, or occupied by the DOC, and every real property that is owned, leased or occupied by the DOC or a community-based program under the DOC jurisdiction or contract.

Judgment- A judgment refers to a certified statement that is signed by a judge which sentences an inmate to a term in prison. It is also known as Judgment of Conviction, Sentence, Commitment Papers or Order (Correctional Glossary of Terms).

Obsessive-Compulsive Disorder- This mental disorder includes some major symptoms such as compulsions and obsessions, which often drive someone to engage in unwanted, and most times distressed, thoughts or behaviors. It is characterized by recurrent thoughts that are disturbing (known as obsessions) as well as repetitive, ritualized behaviors that an individual feel compelled to perform (known as compulsion). Sometimes, it can also be in the form of intrusive images or unwanted impulses. Most people with obsessive-compulsive disorder have obsessions and compulsions, while a 20 percent of minorities may have obsessions or compulsions, but 10 percent may only have one of the diagnosis of obsession or compulsion (Grohol, 2018).

Offender- This is any person that is sentenced or remanded to the custody of the DOC and confined in a jail, prison or any other correctional facility which accommodates individuals that have been convicted of crimes. It includes U.S. marshal holds in the custody of the DOC and Federal inmates, a parolee (inmates under parole or suspended sentence supervision by Parole Services or under parole or the supervision of another state) or a juvenile (that is either in private placement, DOC placement or aftercare) (Correctional Glossary of Terms).

Personality Disorder- This refers to a type of mental disorder that causes people suffering from it to have a rigid and unhealthy way of functioning, thinking and behaving. Individuals with a personality disorder often have issues perceiving and relating to situations and people. Consequently, they have serious problems and limitations in social activities, relationships, and school (Mayo Clinic).

Post-Traumatic Stress Disorder- This is a mental disorder which develops in some individuals that might have witnessed or experienced a scary, shocking, or dangerous event. Although we naturally feel afraid during and after a traumatic event, most people often recover from the initial symptoms of a traumatic situation naturally. However, those that continue to experience the issues after such events may be diagnosed with PTSD. They may feel frightened or stressed even when they are not in any visible danger (National Institute of Mental Health).

Probation- It has to do with adult offenders that the courts have placed under supervision in the community, through a probation agency in place of imprisonment. In some jurisdictions, probationers are sentenced to a combined short-term incarceration sentence which will be followed immediately by probation (which is known as a split sentence) (Bureau of Justice Statistics).

Recidivism- This is known as the percentage of inmates that returns to prison after they are initially released. It has to do with the return of convicted felons to their former criminal ways as a result of committing further crimes. It is not an uncommon phenomenon due to factors such as proclivity to break the law, predisposition to violence, and the external environment they often return to outside of prison. Recidivists often commit crimes against property (especially burglary and theft) since they are commonly faced with the challenge of getting employed and living a decent life (U.S Correctional System).

Re-entry Program- This is an institutional-based program that is made up of intensive case management, job assistance programs, cognitive behavior programs and money management for offenders who have a high-risk of reoffending.

Sex Offender- All adult offenders that have been convicted or adjudicated of a sex crime as listed in SDCL 22-24B-1, no matter the date of the offense or the conviction date. It is also an offender that is currently serving a prison term as a condition of a suspended imposition of sentence for committing a sex crime and offenders that have a history of being sexually abusive or violent behavior (which includes sexually abusive or violent behavior while they were incarcerated) or a factual basis exists that a crime that they were charged for or convicted/adjudicated of involves sexual abuse or sexual violence and have been recognized as having Sexual Behavior Issue (SBI) (designated by sexual behavior code 2) (Corrections Glossary of Terms).

Schizophrenia- This is a mental disorder which often occurs in late adolescence or early adulthood, and it is characterized by hallucinations, delusions, and other cognitive difficulties. It can be a lifelong struggle (Nordqvist, 2017).

Symptomatic Expression- Emotional or interpersonal maladjustment especially in children (as by nail-biting, enuresis, negativism, or by overt hostile or antisocial acts)

Suicide Watch- Potentially suicidal inmates that are in a DOC institution are safely kept in a segregation cell on constant observation or close observation level.

Trans-institutionalization- It is a process whereby people who are assumed deinstitutionalized due to community care policies, in practice end up in other institutions instead of their own homes. For instance, individuals who are mentally ill that are discharged from mental hospitals are often found in prisons, homes for the elderly, nursing homes, and boarding houses (Encyclopedia).

Violent Offenders- These are offenders presently serving a sentence for a conviction of a crime of violence. Conspiracy, attempt, aiding and abetting are also counted as the same principle felony (Correctional Glossary of Terms).

Mental disorders are often associated with issues that individuals experience with their mind and mood. In terms of their causes, they are not properly understood, and yet, the symptoms of mental illnesses are scientifically valid and well-known (Grohol, 2018). Mental illness has continued to be a major issue in prisons and among criminals in the

United States. If the population of individuals incarcerated in prisons is to be reduced, then it is important to improve rehabilitative services as well as mental illness treatments in this dangerous yet vulnerable population (Forensics College).

Some types of severe mental illness actually increase the risk that an individual will engage in violent crime. Although risks vary based on other factors like unemployment and substance abuse, the majority of the risks are actually from secondary effects of mental illness. For instance, getting a job would be hard or even impossible for someone with cognitive difficulties. It could have been possible to prevent some of the notorious mass murders earlier mentioned here and several others if people that knew about very dangerous individuals had provided the information to the right authorities. Assisting individuals with severe mental illness is expensive, but also compassionate and is definitely one of the best long-term investments that can be made in our society (Kopel, 2015).

Final Thoughts

History is filled with records of several inmates who had mental illnesses. In April of 1993, Amanda Wallace stuffed a stock in her 3-year-old son's mouth (Joseph Wallace) and put him on a chair. She proceeded to wave goodbye to him before hanging him using an electrical cord from the transom above a door in her apartment on Chicago's West Side.

Although John Wayne Gacy was an outgoing and sociable young adult, a married man and father, he was also a ruthless predator. It was recorded that he tortured, raped and strangled 33 young men between 1972 and 1978 before he was finally arrested. He was not remorseful, even during his last moment; the final words of Gacy before he was executed by lethal injection on May 10, 1994, were, "Kiss my ass." Even after his arrest and incarceration, for several reasons, some of Gacy's victims have yet to be identified (Bonn, 2014 & Dart, 2017).

Actually, one of the challenges that correctional officers, staff, and public defenders working for Cook County Jail (which includes the city of Chicago) are facing is what has been described as nightmare levels of sexual assault and harassment. This was based on a lawsuit that was filed in Illinois federal court by six female lawyers. Male prisoners in both courtroom lockups as well as the Cook County Jail, on several occasions, had exposed themselves and even masturbated in front of law clerks, interns, and lawyers. This issue made it almost impossible for them to carry out their jobs (Peck, 2017).

This trend made it quite difficult for lawyers to communicate with clients, making it challenging for them to work when other inmates are exposing their genitals, flaccid or erect, and masturbating while they either stare at the lawyers or yell at them to look. As a matter of fact, in the first ten months of the year, 222 detainees in Cook County were charged with indecent exposure. The victims of such indecent acts worked at the jail, and many failed to file complaints because they were afraid of retaliation. According to Cook County Public Defender, Amy Campanelli,

> *"Our attorneys are being forced to work in an environment that is traumatizing and debilitating. These attacks have also affected the safety of the workplace."*
>
> (Peck, 2017)

The possibility that mentally ill inmates will end up back in jail is often high, and they remain in jail for a longer period of time than other inmates. They are more likely to violate prison rules, which further lowers their chances of obtaining a reduction in their sentence for possible good behavior. According to the results of a study that focused on discovering the level of violation of prison rules by inmates, it was observed that inmates with mental illnesses in correctional facilities were twice as likely to be charged with the violation of facility rules, at 19 percent in comparison to 9 percent (Turner, 2007; Butterfield, 2003; Connolly, 2011 and Criminal Justice/Mental Consensus Project).

Treating individuals with serious mental illnesses is a challenging and complex endeavor. Serious mental illness has now become so prevalent in the US corrections system that correctional facilities have come to be regarded as the "new asylums." Actually, Chicago's Cook County Jail, New York's Riker's Island Jail, and Los Angeles County Jail currently have more mentally ill inmates than all the remaining psychiatric hospitals in the US.

About 20 percent of inmates in jails, as well as 15 percent of inmates in state prisons, are now estimated to have a serious mental illness. When we consider the total inmate population, this implies that approximately 383,000 persons with severe psychiatric diseases were behind bars in the US in 2014 (nearly ten times the number of patients found in the nation's state hospitals). In US correctional facilities, the leading cause of death is suicide; multiple studies reveal that as many as half of all inmate suicides are actually committed by an estimate of 15 to 20 percent of inmates with serious mental illness.

As a result of their impaired thinking, inmates having serious mental illnesses also present behavioral management issues, which greatly contributes to their massive over-representation in the subset of inmates in solitary confinement. According to the results of a 2010 audit of three state prisons, between 55 percent and 76 percent of inmates in segregation (solitary confinement) are mentally ill (Treatment Advocacy Center, 2016).

References

Abram, K. M., Teplin, L. A, McClelland, G. M., and Dulcan, M. K. (2003). Comorbid Psychiatric Disorders in Youth in Juvenile Detention. Archives of General Psychiatry. 2003; 60:1097–1108.

Abramsky, S., and Fellner, J. (2003). Ill-equipped: US prisons and offenders with mental illness. Human Rights Watch, pp 145– 68.

Abramson, M. F. (1972) The criminalization of mentally disordered behavior: possible side-effect of a new mental health law, Hospital and Community Psychiatry 1972; 23: 101–105. (New York: Oxford University Press, 2013).

Accreditation Council for Graduate Medical Education. ACGME program requirements for graduate medical education in forensic psychiatry. Available at: http://www.acgme.org/acWebsite/downloads/RRC_progReq/406pr703_u105.pdf. Accessed December 30, 2010.

Adams, K., & Ferrandino, J. (2008). Managing mentally ill inmates in prisons. Criminal Justice and Behavior. 2008; 35 (8):913–927.

Alexander, A., and Gavin, O. (2018). Staff keeps quitting at NC's toughest prisons. It's critically dangerous. The Charlotte Observer.

Amadeo, K. (2018). Deinstitutionalization, It's Causes, Effects, Pros, and Cons. How Deinstitutionalization in the 1970s Affects You Today.

American Psychiatric Association. What is Mental Illness.

American Psychiatric Association, 1994. Diagnostic and Statistical Manual of Mental Disorders, 4th ed. Washington D.C.

American Psychiatric Association. (2000). Psychiatric Services in

Jails and Prisons, 2nd Ed. (Washington D.C., American Psychiatric Association, 2000).

American Psychiatric Association. (2000). Task Force Report no. 29, Psychiatric Services to Jails and Prisons (Washington, DC: American Psychiatric Association, 2nd ed., 2000).

American Psychiatric Association. (2012). Position statement on segregation of prisoners with mental illness. Arlington, VA.

Andre, G., Pease, K., Kendall, K., and Boulton, A. (1994). Health and Offence Histories of Young Offenders in Saskatoon, Canada. Criminal Behaviour and Mental Health. 1994; 4:163–180.

Appelbaum, K. L., Hickey, J. M., and Packer, I. (2001). The Role of Correctional Officers in Multidisciplinary Mental Health Care in Prisons.

Appelbaum, K. L. et al. (1997). Report on the Psychiatric Management of John Salvi in Massachusetts Department of Correction Facilities 1995-1996, submitted to the Massachusetts Department of Correction, January 31, 1997.

Appelbaum, K.L. (2009). Attention deficit hyperactivity disorder in prison: a treatment protocol. J Am Acad Psychiatry Law. 2009; 37: 45-49.

Arrigo, B. A., & Bullock, J. L. (2008). The Psychological Effects of Solitary Confinement on Prisoners in Supermax Units, 52 Int'l J. Offender Therapy & Comparative Criminology 622, 628 (summarizing the symptoms associated with Grassian's SHU Syndrome).

Arrigo, B., & Bullock, J. L. (2008). The Psychological Effects of Solitary Confinement on Prisoners in Supermax Units. International Journal of Offender Therapy and Comparative Criminology, 52 (6), 622-40.

Atkins, L., Pumariega, A., Rogers, K., Montgomery, L., Nybro, C., Jeffers, G., and Sease F. (1999). Mental health and incarcerated youth—I: Prevalence and nature of psychopathology. J. Child. Fam. Stud. 1999;8:193–204. doi: 10.1023/A:1022040018365.

Baglivio, M. T., Epps, N., Swartz, K., Sayedul Huq, M., Sheer, A., & Hardt, N. S. (2014). The prevalence of adverse childhood experiences (ACE) in the lives of juvenile offenders. Journal of Juvenile Justice, 3(2).

Baillargeon, J., Binswanger, I. A., Penn, J. V., Williams, B. A., & Murray, O. J. (2009). Psychiatric disorders and repeat incarcerations: the revolving prison door. Am J Psychiatry. 2009; 166 (1):103–109.

Bales, W. D., Nadel, M., Reed, C., & Blomberg, T. G. (2017). Recidivism and Inmate Mental Illness, International Journal of Criminology and Sociology. Lifescience Global, 2017.

Basoglu, M., Livanou, M., & Crnobaric, C. (2007). Torture vs. other cruel, inhuman and degrading treatment: is the distinction real or apparent? Arch Gen Psychiatry 64:277– 85.

Belcher, J. R. (1988). Are jails replacing the mental health system for the homeless mentally ill? Community Mental Health Journal 1988; 24:185–195.

Belluck, P. (2007). Mentally ill inmates at risk in isolation, lawsuit says, New York Times, Mar. 9, 2007.

Bender, E. (2003). Community treatment more humane, reduces criminal-justice costs, Psychiatric News, 38, 28.

Bernd, C., Mitra, A. N., and Loftus-Farren, Z. (2017). America's Toxic Prisons: The Environmental Injustices of Mass Incarceration.

Beven, G. (2005). Offenders with Mental Illnesses in Maximum- and Super maximum- Security Settings. Handbook of Correctional Mental Health (2nd Edition). Washington, DC: American Psychiatric Publishing, Inc.

BJS, Prisoners. (2002). In 2002, according to BJS estimates of the capacity of state prison systems.

Black, D. (2017). Antisocial Personality Disorder. Psych Central.

Bowring v. Godwin, 551 F.2d. 44, 47 (4th Cir. 1977).

Bonn, S. A. (2014). John Wayne Gacy: The Diabolical "Killer Clown." Psychology Today.

Bressert, S. (2017). Avoidant Personality Disorder. Psych Central.

Bromberg, W. and Thompson, C. B. (1937). The relation of psychosis, mental defect and personality types to crime, Journal of Criminal Law and Criminology 1937; 28:70–88.

Brown, J. (2013). ACLU uncovers increased proportion of mentally ill inmates in solitary, Denver Post, July 23, 2013.

Bureau of Justice Statistics (BJS). Terms & Definitions: Corrections.

Butterfield, F. (2003). Study finds hundreds of thousands of inmates mentally ill, New York Times, Oct. 22, 2003.

Burns, K. A. (2011). Psychiatry behind bars: Practicing in jails and prisons.

Byron, R. (2014). Criminals Need Mental Health Care: Psychiatric treatment is far better than imprisonment for reducing recidivism, Scientific American.

California Department of Corrections. (2002). Health Care Placement Unit, "Mental Health Adseg/SHU/PSU," population chart created on July 25, 2002.

Christopher, P. P., McCabe, P. J., & Fisher, W. H. (2012). Prevalence of involvement in the criminal justice system during severe mania and associated symptomatology. Psychiatric Services 63:33-39.

Cocozza, J., and Skowyra, K. (2000). Youth with mental health disorders: Issues and emerging responses. Off. Juv. Justice Delinquency Prev. J. 2000; 7:3–13.

Colvin, M., Cullen, F. & Vander Ven, T. (2002). "Coercion, Social Support, and Crime: An Emerging Theoretical Consensus." Criminology, 40: 19ö42.

Condelli, W. S., Dvoskin, J. A., & Holanchock, H. (1994). Intermediate care programs for inmates with psychiatric disorders.

Bulletin of the American Academy of Psychiatry and the La 22:63-70, 1994.

Conklin, G. H. (2000). Family Ties, Depression and Adjustment of Women in Prison in North Carolina. Retrieved September 22, 2015, from http://www.ncsociology.org/prison.htm.

Connolly, K. (2011). Mentally ill increasing strain on US prison system, BBC News, Feb. 22, 2011. Convention against Torture and Other Cruel, Inhuman or Degrading Treatment or Punishment. Available at http://www1.umn.edu/humanrts/instree/h2catoc.htm. Accessed January 29, 2010.

Corley, C. (2018). North Dakota Prison Officials Think outside the Box to Revamp Solitary Confinement, npr.

Cormier, B. (1973). The practice of psychiatry in the prison society. Bulletin of the American Academy of Psychiatry and the Law 1:156-183, 1973.

Correctional Association of New York. (1988). "Mental Health in the House of Corrections," forthcoming publication, p. 14; Eng v. Coughlin, 80-CV-385S, 1988 U.S. Dist. LEXIS 18327 (W. D. N.Y., January 29, 1988).

Corrections Glossary of Terms.

Correctionalofficeredu.org. what is a Correctional Officer?

Corrigan, P. W., & Watson, A. C. (2005). Findings from the National Comorbidity Survey on the frequency of violent behavior in individuals with psychiatric disorders. Psychiatry Research 136:153–162.

Council of State Governments, Consensus Project (2002).

Council of State Governments. (2002). Criminal Justice/Mental Health Consensus Project. New York: Author.

Council of State Governments, New York. (2002). Numbers calculated by the Council of State Governments, Criminal Justice/Mental

Health Consensus Project (Council of State Governments, New York, June 2002).

Crepeau, M. (2018). Troubled detainee at center of unusual court fight between Loyola Hospital, Cook County. Chicago Tribune.

Crime Times. (2003). Linking Brain Dysfunction to Disordered/Criminal/psychopathic behavior Vol. 9, No. 4, 2003 Page 8.

Criminal Justice/Mental Health Consensus Project, Fact Sheet: Mental illness and jails.

Culbertson, R. (1977). Personnel conflicts in jail management. American Journal of Corrections 39:28-39, 1977.

Cumming, R., & Solway, H. (1973). The incarcerated psychiatrist. Hospital and Community Psychiatry 24:631-632, 1973.

Daifotis, K. (2018). "Mental Health in U.S. Prisons: How Our System Is Set Up For Failure". CMC Senior Theses. 1784.

Daniel, A. E. (2007). Care of the Mentally Ill in Prisons: Challenges and Solutions. Journal of the American Academy of Psychiatry and the Law Online Dec 2007, 35 (4) 406-410.

Dart, T. J. (2017). Unidentified Victims of John Wayne Gacy; Cook County Sheriff's Office.

Dearen, J. (2005). Mental patients languish in jail, Oakland Tribune (CA), Sept. 22, 2005.

Declaration of Dr. Stuart Grassian, Eng v. Coughlin, 80-CV-385S (W.D. New York) (undated).

Deutsch, A. (1937). The Mentally Ill in America (New York: Doubleday, Doran and Co., 1937), 42.

Diagnostic and statistical manual of mental disorders (4th ed., text rev.). Washington, DC; 2000.

Ditton, P. M. (1999). Mental Health and Treatment of Inmates and Probationers (Washington, DC: Bureau of Justice Statistics Special Report, US Department of Justice, July 1999).

Draine, J. (2003). "Where is the Illness in the Criminalization of the Mentally Ill?" In W.H.

Drapkin, M. (2003). Jails are not designed as care facilities for those with mental disorders, but in fact many jails today are the largest inpatient mental health institutions in the United States.

Drapkin, M. (2003). Management and Supervision of Jail Inmates with Mental Disorders (New Jersey, Civic Research Institute).

Eaton, W. W., Martins, S. S., Nestadt, G., Bienvenu, O. J., Clarke, D., & Alexandre, P. (2008). The burden of mental disorders. Epidemiol Rev. 2008; 30 (1):1–14.

Element Behavioral Health. (2017). Prisoners at Higher Risk for PTSD. Encyclopedia. Trans-institutionalization.

Faiver, K. L. (1998). Organizational issues: corrections and health care: working together, in Health Care Management Issues in Corrections. Edited by Faiver KL. Lanham, Md, American Correctional Association, 1998.

Fazel, S., Hayes, A. J., Bartellas, K., Clerici, M., & Trestman, R. (2016). The mental health of prisoners: a review of prevalence, adverse outcomes and interventions. The Lancet. Psychiatry, 3 (9), 871–881.

Fellner, J. (2006). A corrections quandary: mental illness and prison rules. Harv CR-CL L Rev 41:391– 412.

Fields, G. (2006). No way out: trapped by rules, the mentally ill languish in prison, Wall Street Journal, May 3, 2006.

Fisher, N. (2015) 4 Things To Understand About Youth, Mental Health & Juvenile Justice In The US

Forensics College. Dangerous Minds: The Mental Illnesses of Infamous Criminals.

Fried C., and Reppucci, D. (2001). Criminal decision making: The development of adolescent judgment, criminal responsibility and culpability. Law Hum. Behav. 2001; 25:45–61. doi: 10.1023/A:1005639909226.

Garascia, J. A. (2005). The price we are willing to pay for punitive justice in the juvenile justice system: Mentally ill delinquents and their disproportionate share of the burden. Indiana Law J. 2005;80:489–515.

Geoffroy, P. A., Etain, B., Scott, J., et al. (2013). Reconsideration of bipolar disorder as a developmental disorder: importance of the time of onset. Journal of Physiology, Paris 107:278–285.

Gerstein, M., & Oosting, J. (2016). Growth of mentally ill inmates raises concern in Mich, The Detroit News.

Glaze, L. E, & Herberman, E. J. (2013). Correctional Populations in the United States, 2012. Washington, DC: Bureau of Justice Statistics; 2013.

Glaze, L.E. & James, D.J. (2006). *Mental Health Problems of Prison and Jail Inmates.* Bureau of Justice Statistics Special Report. U.S. Department of Justice, Office of Justice Programs Washington, D.C.

Goss, R. J., Peterson, K., Smith, L. W. et al. (2002). Characteristics of suicide attempts in a large urban jail system with an established suicide prevention program, Psychiatric Services 2002;53: 574–79.

Gottschlich, A.J. & Cetnar, G. (2002). Drug bills at jail top food costs. Springfield News Sun 2002, August 20).

Grant, B. F., Stinson, F.S., Hasin, D.S., et al. (2005). Prevalence, correlates, and comorbidity of bipolar I disorder and axis I and II disorders: results from the National Epidemiologic Survey on Alcohol and Related Conditions. Journal of Clinical Psychiatry 66:1205–1215. Grob, Mental Institutions, 97.

Grisso, T. (2008). Adolescent offenders with mental disorders. Future Child. 2008; 18:143–164. doi: 10.1353/foc.0.0016.

Grob, G. N. (1966). The State and the Mentally Ill (Chapel Hill: University of North Carolina Press, 1966), 24.

Grohol, J. (2018). Obsessive-Compulsive Disorder. Psych Central.

Grohol, J. (2018). Depression. Psych Central.

Grohol, J. (2018). Symptoms & Treatments of Mental Disorders. Psych Central.

Hammel, P. (2016). Nebraska prisons lack staff to improve mental health treatment for inmates, officials say.

Hammond, S. (2007). Mental Health Needs of Juvenile Offenders. National Conference of State Legislatures.

Harold, G., Kerr, D., van Ryzin, M., DeGarmo, D., Rhoades, K., and Leve L. (2013). Depressive symptom trajectories among girls in the juvenile justice system: 24-Month Outcomes of an RCT of Multidimensional Treatment Foster Care. Pre. Sci. 2013;14:437–446. doi: 10.1007/s11121-012-0317-y.

Harrison, P. M., and Karberg, J. C. (2003). Prison and Jail Inmates at Midyear 2002 (Washington D.C.: Bureau of Justice Statistics, April 2003), table 7.

Heilbrun, K., & Griffin, P. A. (1993). "Community-based Treatment of Insanity Acquitees." International Journal of Law and Psychiatry 16: 1ö18.

Heilbrun, K., Lee, R., and Cottle, C. (2005).Risk Factors and Intervention Outcomes: Meta-Analyses of Juvenile Offending. In: Heilbrun K., Goldstein N., Redding R., editors. Juvenile Delinquency: Prevention, Assessment, and Treatment. Oxford University Press; Oxford, UK: 2005.

Hermes, A. (2007). Boone County struggles to meet mental health care needs for inmates, Missourian, Dec. 17, 2007.

HG.org. What is the Difference Between Jail and Prison?

Hill, C. (2004). Inmate mental health care. Correct Compend 29:15–31.

Hilliard, W. T., Barloon, L., Farley, P. et al. (2013). Bupropion diversion and misuse in the correctional facility. J Correct Health Care. 2013; 19: 211-217.

Hills, H., Siegfried, C., and Ickowitz, A. (2004). Effective Prison Mental Health Services: Guidelines to Expand and Improve Treatment. Washington, DC: US Department of Justice, National Institute of Corrections; 2004.

Hornbeck, M. (1977). Mentally ill flood prisons, Detroit News, Dec. 4, 1997.

Houston Behavioral Healthcare Hospital. (2016). The Government's Role in Keeping the Mentally Ill out of Prison.

HUD. (2010). U.S. Department of Housing and Urban Development's (HUD) 2010 Annual Homeless Assessment Report (AHAR) to Congress.

Human Rights Watch. (1997). Cold Storage: Super-Maximum-Security Confinement in Indiana (New York: Human Rights Watch, 1997), p. 34.

Human Rights Watch. (2002). interview with Gloria Henry, warden, Valley State Prison for Women, California, July 17, 2002.

Human Rights Watch. (2002). Human Rights Watch visited Graterford, August 12, 2002.

Human Rights Watch. (2002). Human Rights Watch telephone interview with Gary Fields, administrator, Counseling and Treatment Services, Oregon Department of Corrections, June 24, 2002.

Human Rights Watch. (2002). Interview with Sandra Schank, staff psychiatrist, Mule Creek State Prison, California, July 19, 2002.

Human Rights Watch. (2003). Ill-Equipped: U.S. Prisons and Offenders with Mental Illness, Printed in the United States of America. ISBN: 1564322904.

Human Rights Watch. (2003). Ill-Equipped: Email communication from Dr. Terry.

Human Rights Watch. (2003). Ill-Equipped: U.S. Prisons and

Offenders with Mental Illness, Printed in the United States of America. ISBN: 1564322904.

Human Rights Watch. (2003). Ill-Equipped: U.S. Prisons and Offenders with Mental.

Human Rights Watch. (2003). Interview with Dave Munson, head psychologist, McNeil Island Correctional Center, Washington, August 22, 2002.

Human Rights Watch. (2003). Kupers to Human Rights Watch, May 29, 2003. U.S. Prisons and Offenders with Mental Illness, Printed in the United States of America. ISBN: 1564322904.

Ibid. Human Rights Watch (2003).

Interim Report of the Special Rapporteur on Torture and Other Cruel, Inhuman or Degrading Treatment or Punishment. (2008). UN General Assembly. New York: United Nations, UN Doc. A/63/175:18 –21, 2008.

International Covenant on Civil and Political Rights. (2010). Available at http://www1.umn.edu/humanrts/instree/b3ccpr.htm. Accessed January 29, 2010.

James, D. J. and Glaze, L. E. (2006) Mental Health Problems of Prison and Jail Inmates (Washington, DC: Bureau of Justice Statistics, US Department of Justice, NCJ 213600, Sept. 2006).

Jeffrey, L., Metzner, M. D., and Fellner, J. (2010). Solitary Confinement and Mental Illness in U.S. Prisons: A Challenge for Medical Ethics.

Jenkins, J. (2017). Arizona Prison Health Care Contract Leads To 'Severe Understaffing,' Kjzz.

Jones 'El v. Berge, 164 F. Supp.2d 1096, 1108 (W.D. Wis., 2001).

Kamperman, A. M., Henrichs, J., Bogaerts, S., et al. (2014). Criminal victimization in people with severe mental illness: a multi-site prevalence and incidence survey in the Netherlands. PLoS ONE 9:e91029.

Kaufman, E. (1973). Can comprehensive mental health care be

provided in an overcrowded prison system? Journal of Psychiatry and the Law 1:243-262, 1973.

Keers, R., Ullrich, S., DeStavola, B. L. et al. (2014). Association of violence with emergence of persecutory delusions in untreated schizophrenia, American Journal of Psychiatry 2014; 171:332–339.

Kessler, R. C., Berglund, P., Dember, O., Jin, R., Merikangas, K. R., Walters, E. E. (2005) Lifetime prevalence and age-of-onset distributions of DSM-IV disorders in the National Comorbidity Survey Replication.

Khazan, O. (2015). Most Prisoners are Mentally Ill: Can mental-health courts, in which people are sentenced to therapy, help? The Atlantic.

Knoll, J. (2006). A tale of two crises: mental health treatment in corrections. J Dual Diagnosis 3:7–21, 2006.

Kopel, D. (2015). Facts about mental illness and crime, The Washington Post.

Kupers, T. (1999). Prison Madness, 1999.

Lamb, H.R., Weinberger, L.E., & Gross, B.H. (1999). "Community Treatment of Severely Mental Ill Offenders under the Jurisdiction of the Criminal Justice System: A Review." Psychiatric Services 50: 907ö913.

Lamb, H. R., Weinberger, L. E. (2016). Rediscovering the Concept of Asylum for Persons with Serious Mental Illness. Journal of the American Academy of Psychiatry and the Law Online March 2016.

Lamb, R., & Weinberger, L. (2005). The Shift of Psychiatric Inpatient Care from Hospitals to Jails and Prisons. The Journal of the American Academy of Psychiatry and the Law, 33(4), 529-34.

Lee, M.A. (2015). Mental Health Services and the American Inmate: A Systematic Review of Literature Master of Social Work Clinical Research Papers. Paper 482. Mayo Clinic, Personality Disorders.

Leve, L., and Chamberlain, P. (2007). A randomized evaluation of multidimensional treatment foster care: Effects on school attendance and homework completion in juvenile justice girls. Res. Soc. Work Pract. 2007;17:657–663. doi: 10.1177/1049731506293971.

Lewis, A. Incarceration and Mental Health, Center for Prisoner Health and Human Rights.

Loeber, R., and Keenan, K. (1994). Interaction between conduct disorder and its comorbid conditions: Effects of age and gender. Clin. Psychol. Rev. 1994;14:497–523. doi: 10.1016/0272-7358(94)90015-9.

López, M., and Maiello-Reidy, L. (2017). Prisons and the mentally ill: why design matters, Penal Reform International.

Lovell, D., Gagliardi, G.J., & Peterson, P.D. (2002). "Recidivism and the Use of Services Among Persons with Mental Illness After Release from Prison." Psychiatric Services 53: 1290ö1296.

Lovell, D. (2008). Patterns of disturbed behavior in a supermax prison.

Lovell, D., Cloyes, K., Allen, D., & Rhodes, L. (2000). "Who Lives in Super-Maximum Custody? A Washington State Study," Federal Probation, vol. 64, no. 2, Dec. 2000.

Lund, B. C., Flaum, M., Adam, L. A. et al., (2002). Psychiatric prescribing trends and practices in Iowa prisons, Psychiatric Services 2002; 53:1023–24.

Lurigio, A. J. (2002). "Coerced Drug Treatment for Offenders: Does It Work?" GLATTC Research Update 4: 1ö2.

Lurigio, A. J., Rollins, A., and Fallon, J. (n.d). The Effects of Serious Mental Illness on Offender Reentry, Federal Probation a Journal of Correctional philosophy and practice. Volume 68 number 2.

Lyden, T. (2012). KMSP-TV bio/email, Feb. 26, 2013.

Madrid v. Gomez, 889 F. Supp. 1146, 1265 (N.D. Cal. 1995).

Mason, N. (2007). Setting the Stage - A Brief History of Detention Centers and Mental Illness in the United States. Correctional Psychiatry: Practice Guidelines and Strategies. Kingston,

NJ: Civic Research Institute.

Maue, F. (2002). Human Rights Watch interview with Dr. Fred Maue, chief of clinical services, Pennsylvania Department of Corrections, Gaudenzia House, Philadelphia, Pennsylvania, August 13, 2002.

Mayo Clinic. Schizophrenia.

Mears, D. P., & Cochran, J. C. (2012). U.S. prisoner reentry health care policy in international perspective: service gaps and the moral and public health implications. Prison J. 2012; 92 (2):175–202.

Mental Health America, (2015). Position Statement 51: Children With Emotional Disorders In The Juvenile Justice System. Retrieved on September 7Th 2017 from

Merriam Webster Dictionary.

Metzner, J.L., Cohen, F., Grossman L.S., et al: Treatment in jails and prisons, in Treatment of Offenders with Mental Disorders. Edited by Wettstein RM. New York, Guilford, 1998.

Metzner, J. L. (1993). Guidelines for psychiatric services in prisons, Criminal Behavior and Mental Health 1993 3:252–67.

Metzner, J. L. (1998). An introduction to correctional psychiatry: part III. Journal of the American Academy of Psychiatry and the Law 26:107-115, 1998.

Metzner, J. L., and Dvoskin, J. A. (2006). An overview of correctional psychiatry. Psychiatr Clin North Am 29:761–72.

Metzner, J. L., and Fellner, J. (2010). Solitary Confinement and Mental Illness in U.S. Prisons: A Challenge for Medical Ethics.

Miller, C.M. & Fantz, A. (2007). Special "psych" jails planned, Miami Herald (2007, November 15).

Murray, C., & Lopez, A. (1996). The Global Burden of Disease.

A Comprehensive Assessment of Morbidity and Disability from Diseases, Injuries and Risk Factors in 1990 and Projected to 2020. Cambridge, Mass, Harvard University Press.

Nordqvist, C. (2017). Understanding the symptoms of schizophrenia, Medical News Today.

National Alliance on Mental Illness. (NAMI) Mental Health by the Numbers.

National Institute of Corrections. (2001). Provision of Mental Health Care in Prisons.

National Institute of Mental Health. (NIH). Bipolar Disorder.

National Institute of Mental Health. Post-Traumatic Stress Disorder.

National Institute of Mental Health. (2017). Transforming the Understanding and Treatment of Mental Illness.

National Mental Health Association (NMHA), (2004). In: Mental Health Treatment for Youth in The Juvenile Justice System: A Compendium of Promising Practices. John D., Catherine T., editors. MacArthur Foundation; Chicago, IL, USA: 2004.

National Resource Center on Homelessness and Mental Illness. (2003). Get the Facts.

NCMHJJ. (2007). National Center for Mental Health and Juvenile Justice. *Blueprint for Change: A Comprehensive Model for the Identification and Treatment of Youth with Mental Health Needs in Contact with the Juvenile Justice System.* Delmar, N.Y: Skowyra, K.R. & Cocozza, J.J. Retrieved January 16, 2015.

New Freedom Commission on Mental Health. (2002). Interim Report of the President's New Freedom Commission on Mental Health, October 29, 2002.

NIMH. (n.d.). Retrieved September 22, 2015, from https://www.nimh.nih.gov/health/statistics/major depression.shtml.

Nurse, J., Woodcock, P., & Ormsby, J. (2003). Influence of

environmental factors on mental health within prisons: Focus group study. BMJ (Clinical research ed.). 327. 480. 10.1136/bmj.327.7413.480.

Okasha, A. (2004). Mental patients in prisons: punishment versus treatment? World Psychiatry, 3 (1), 1-2.

O'Keefe, M., & Schnell, M. J. (2007). Offenders with Mental Illness in the Correctional System. Journal of Offender Rehabilitation, 45(1-2), 81-104.

Open Society Foundations. (2015). What Is Deinstitutionalization?

Ovalle, D. (2013). Police probing Miami-Dade death of mentally ill inmate, Miami Herald, July 26, 2013.

Parker, G. (2009). Impact of a Mental Health Training Course for Correctional Officers on a Special Housing Unit. Psychiatric Services, 60(5), 640-45.

Parker, M. (2010). Mentally ill jailed, awaiting therapy, Clarion Ledger (Jackson, MS), Aug. 16, 2010.

PBS. (2014). By the numbers: Mental illness behind bars.

Peck, E. (2017). Huff Posts U.S. News Masturbating Inmates Are a 'Traumatizing' Daily Problem for Female Lawyers in This Jail.

Pittaro, M. (2015). The Challenges of Incarcerating Mentally Ill Inmates, In Public Safety.

Powelson, H., & Bendix, R. (1951). Psychiatry in prison. Psychiatry 14:73-86.

Psychology Today. (2018). Depressive Disorders.

Ptacin, M. (2017). Guards vs. Inmates: Mistreatment and Abuse in the US Prison System. Publication No. (SMA) 15-4927. Rockville, MD: Substance Abuse and Mental Health Services Administration.

Pulay, A. J., Dawson, D. A., Hasin, D. S., et al. (2008). Violent behavior and DSM-IV psychiatric disorders: results from the National

Epidemiologic Survey on Alcohol and Related Conditions. Journal of Clinical Psychiatry 69: 12–22.

Quanbeck, C. D., Stone, D. C., McDermott, B. E., et al. (2005). Relationship between criminal arrest and community treatment history among patients with bipolar disorder. Psychiatric Services 56:847–852.

Ranker Crime. (n.d). 9 Serial Killers Who Suffered From Mental Illness; Ranker.

Rathbun, A. (2009). Inmates with mental illness bring extra costs to Monroe Prison, Everett (WA) Herald, Nov. 23, 2009.

Reyes, H. (2007). The worst scars are in the mind: psychological torture. Int Rev Red Cross 89:591– 617.

Report on the Status of Assisted Outpatient Treatment (New York State Office of Mental Health, March 2005).

Roberts, R., Atkins, C., and Rosenblatt A. (1998). Prevalence of psychopathology among children and adolescents. Am. J. Psychiatry. 1998;155:715–725.

Roth, L. (1986). Correctional psychiatry, in Forensic Psychiatry and Psychology: Perspectives and Standards for Interdisciplinary Practice. Edited by Curran WJ, McGarry AL, Shah SA. Philadelphia, Davis, 1986.

Roth-Rochester, C. (2017). How to Keep People with Mental Illness out of Prison, Futurity.

Ruiz v. Estelle, 503 F. Supp 1265 (S.D. Tex. 1980).

Ruiz v. Estelle, 503 F. Supp. at 1336.

Ruiz v. Johnson, 37 F. Supp. 2d 855, 914 (S.D. Texas, 1999), rev'd 178 F.3d 385 (5th Cir. Tex., 1999), adhered to on remand, 243 F.3d 941 (5th Cir. Tex., 2001).

SAMHSA. (2014). Behavioral Health Trends in the United States: Results from the 2014 National Survey on Drug Use and Health. *Mental Health Findings*, NSDUH Series H-50, HHS

Sahlin, J. (2018). The Prison Problem: Recidivism Rates and Mental Health, Good Therapy.

Sartx, Blazer, George & Winfield. (1990). "Estimating the Prevalence of Borderline Personality in the Community," Journal of Personality Disorders, vol. 4, no. 3 (1990).

Schoenly, L. (n.d). Scope and Standards: Five Correctional Nurse Roles, Correctional Nurse.

Scottsdale, B. (n. d). What is a Prison Psychiatrist, the Nest.

Scott-Hayward, C. S. (2009). The Fiscal Crisis in Corrections: Rethinking Policies and Practices. New York, NY: Vera Institute of Justice; 2009.

Sacramento Bee, March 17, 1999 to "Treatment Not Jail" Sacramento Bee, March 17, 1999, "on any given day, Los Angeles County Jail holds as many as 3,300 seriously mentally ill" people.

Sickmund M. (2004) Juveniles in corrections. Juvenile offenders and victims national report series. Washington, DC: Office of Juvenile Justice and Delinquency Prevention; 2004.

Shelton, D. (2005). Patterns of treatment services and costs for young offenders with mental disorders. J. Child. Adolesc. Psych. Nurs. 2005;18:103–112. doi: 10.1111/j.1744-6171.2005.00013.x.

Simmons, A. (2006). Prisons see more inmates requiring mental health care, Gwinnett (GA) Daily Post, July 30, 2006; Jail situation is insane (editorial), Rome (GA) News Tribune, Dec. 19, 2011.

Simpson, J. R. (2014). Correctional Psychiatry: Challenges and Rewards, Psychiatric Times.

Skowyra, K. R. & Cocozza, J.J., (2007). Blueprint for Change: A Comprehensive Model for the Identification and Treatment of Youth with Mental Health Needs in Contact with the Juvenile Justice System. Delmar, NY: National Center for Mental Health and Juvenile Justice (2007).

Slaughter, E. (2016). Preschool To Prison. Is it Determined By The School, Environment, or Parent?

Smith, P. S. (2006). The Effects of Solitary Confinement on Prison Inmates: A Brief History and Review of the Literature, 34 Crime & Justice 441, 486.

Soderstrom, I. (2007). Mental Illness in Offender Populations: Prevalence, Duty and Implications. Journal of Offender Rehabilitation, 45(1-2), 1-17.

State of Maine, 120th Legislature, Final Report of the Committee to Study the Needs of Persons with Mental Illness Who Are Incarcerated, December 19, 2001, introduction, p. ii, accessed from http://www.state.me.us/legis/opla/incarrept.PDF, on June 23, 2003.

Statistics Canada. Youth Court Statistics 2002–2003. Ottawa, ON: Canadian Centre for Justice Statistics; 2004.

Stoddard-Dare, P., Mallett, C., and Boitel, C. (2011). Association between mental health disorders and juveniles' detention for a personal crime. Child. Adolesc. Ment. Health. 2011;16:208–213. doi: 10.1111/j.1475-3588.2011.00599.x.

Substance Abuse and Mental Health Services Administration, *Results from the 2014 National Survey on Drug Use and Health: Mental Health Findings*, NSDUH Series H-50, HHS Publication No. (SMA) 15-4927. Rockville, MD: Substance Abuse and Mental Health Services Administration. (2015).

Swanson, J. W., Borum, R., Swartz, M. S. et al. (2001). Can involuntary outpatient commitment reduce arrests among persons with severe mental illness? Criminal Justice and Behavior 2001;28: 156-89.

Takeda, Y. (2000). Aggression in relation to childhood depression: A study of Japanese 3rd-6th graders. Jpn. J. Dev. Psychol. 2000;11:1–11.

Tamburello, A. C., Lieberman, J. A., Baum, R. M., & Reeves, R. (2012). Successful removal of quetiapine from a correctional formulary. J Am Acad Psychiatry Law. 2012; 40: 502-508.

Teplin, L. A., Abram, K. M., McClelland, G. M., Dulcan, M. K., and Mericle, A. A. (2002). Psychiatric disorders in youth in juvenile detention. Arch. Gen. Psychiatry. 2002;59:1133–1143. doi: 10.1001/archpsyc.59.12.1133.

Temporini, H., Feuerstein, S., Coric, V., Fortunati, F., Southwick, S., & Morgan, C. A. (2006). Correctional Psychiatry. Psychiatry (Edgemont), 3 (1), 26–29.

Temporini, H. (2010). Conducting Mental Health Assessments in Correctional Settings. The Handbook of Correctional Mental Health (2nd Edition). Arlington, VA: American Psychiatric Publishing, Inc.

Thomas, P. (2004). The many forms of bipolar disorder: a modern look at an old illness. Journal of Affective Disorders 79 (suppl 1): S3–S8.

Toch, H. (1975). Men in Crisis: Human Breakdown in Prison (1975).

Toch H., & Adams K. (2002). Acting Out: Maladaptive Behavior in Confinement (Washington D.C.: American Psychological Association, April 2002), p. 16.

Torrey, E. F. (2002). The Insanity Offense (New York: W. W. Norton, 2002); E. Fuller Torrey, American Psychosis.

Torrey, E. F., Kennard, A. D. and Eslinger, D. More. (2010). Mentally Ill Persons Are in Jails and Prisons than Hospitals: A Survey of the States (Arlington, VA: Treatment Advocacy Center, 2010).

Torrey, E.F., Kennard, A.D., Eslinger, D.F., Lamb, H.R., Pavle, J. (2010). More mentally ill persons are in jails and prisons than hospitals: A survey of the states. Arlington, VA: Treatment Advocacy Center.

Torrey, E. F., Stieber, J. and Ezekiel, J. (1992). Criminalizing the Seriously Mentally Ill: The Abuse of Jails as Mental Hospitals (Washington, DC: National Alliance for the Mentally Ill and Public Citizen's Health Research Group, 1992.

Torrey, E.F., Zdanowicz, M.T., Kennard, A.D., Lamb, H.R., Eslinger,

D.F., Biasotti, M.I., Fuller, D.A. (2014). The treatment of persons with mental illness in prisons and jails: A state survey. Arlington, VA: Treatment Advocacy Center.

Treatment Advocacy Center. (2014). The Treatment of Persons with Mental Illness in Prisons and Jails: A State Survey.

Treatment Advocacy Center. (2016). Serious Mental Illness (SMI) Prevalence in Jails and Prisons, A Background Paper from the Office of Research & Public Affairs.

Turner, C. (2007). Ethical issues in criminal justice administration, American Jails 2007; 20:4953.

Uzlen, T. P. M., and Hamilton, H. (1998). The nature and characteristics of psychiatric comorbidity in incarcerated adolescents. Canadian Journal of Psychiatry. 1998; 43:57–63.

Underwood, L. A., Washington, A. (2016). Mental Illness and Juvenile Offenders. Int J Environ Res Public Health. 2016 Feb; 13(2): 228. PMCID: PMC4772248 doi: 10.3390/ijerph13020228.

United Nations Human Rights Committee. (1992). CCPR General comment No. 20: replaces general comment 7 concerning prohibition of torture, or other cruel, inhuman or degrading treatment or punishment. New York: UNHRC, 1992.

United Nations Human Rights Committee. (2006). Consideration of reports submitted by States parties under Article 40 of the Covenant, concluding observations of the Human Rights Committee, United States of America. New York: UNHRC, UN Doc. CCPR/C/USA/CO/3, 2006.

United Nations Committee against Torture. (2006). Consideration of reports submitted by States parties under Article 19 of the Convention, Conclusions and Recommendations of the Committee Against Torture, United States of America. New York: UN Committee against Torture, UN Doc. CAT/C/USA/CO/2, 2006.

U.S Correctional System. The U.S Correctional System Defined.

United States Department of Justice (USDJ), (2011). Department of

Justice Activities under the Civil. Rights Institutionalized Persons Act: Fiscal Year 2010. CRIPA; Washington, DC, USA: 2011.

Van Dorn, R. A., Desmarais, S. L., Petrila, J. et al. (2013). Effects of outpatient treatment on risk of arrest of adults with serious mental illness and associated costs, Psychiatric Services 2013, May 15 [Epub ahead of print].

Varney, S. (2014). By the numbers: Mental Illness Behind Bars, Kaiser Health News

Vicki, A. B. (n.d.). Roles of Correctional Psychologists. Work - Chron.com.

Voskanian, P. (2002). Human Rights Watch interview with Pogos Voskanian, psychiatrist, Gaudenzia House, Philadelphia, Pennsylvania, August 13, 2002.

Wald, J., and Losen, D. (2003). Defining and redirecting a school-to-prison pipeline. New Dir. Youth Dev. 2003;2003:9–15. doi: 10.1002/yd.51.

Washington v. Harper, 494 U.S. 210 (1990)

Wasserman, G. A., McReynolds, L. S., Lucas, C. P., Fisher, P., and Santos L. (2002). The voice DISC-IV with incarcerated male youths: Prevalence of disorder. J. Am. Acad. Child. Adolesc. Psychiatry. 2002;41:314–321. doi: 10.1097/00004583-200203000-00011.

Wilper, A. P., Woolhandler, S., Boyd, J. W et al. (2009). The health and health care of US prisoners: results of a nationwide survey. Am J Public Health. 2009; 99:666–672.

Written communication from Fred Cohen to Human Rights Watch, August 28, 2003.

Wines, F. H. (1888). Report on the Defective, Dependent and Delinquent Classes of the Population of the United States (Washington, DC: Government Printing Office, 1888).

WHO. (2005). Resource Book on Mental Health, Human Rights and Legislation, World Health Organization 2005.

WHO. Mental Health and Prisons: Information Sheet.

Wolff, N., Blitz, C. L., & Shi, J. (2007). Rates of sexual victimization in prison for inmates with and without mental disorders, Psychiatric Services 2007; 58:1087–94.

Wolff, N., Plemmons, D., Veysey, B. et al. (2002). Release planning for inmates with mental illness compared with those who have other chronic illnesses, Psychiatric Services 2002; 53:1469–71.

Zielbauer, P. Von. (2003). Report says many inmates in isolation are mentally ill, New York Times, Oct 22, 2003.

Yoon, J. H., Kim, J. H., Choi, S. S., et al. (2012). Homicide and bipolar I disorder: a 22-year study. Forensic Science International 217:113–118.

Zoukis, C. (2018). Mental Illness Is Rampant In American Jails And Prisons, Huffington Post.

Biography

Elvis Slaughter Sr. is a retired Cook County Sheriff's Superintendent of Corrections/Deputy Sheriff with more than thirty years of experience in criminal justice and law enforcement. Slaughter holds a Master's in Criminal Justice and Corrections. He has authored several articles and ten books, which include *Safer Jail and Prison Matters* and *Preschool to Prison*. Elvis is a speaker, security consultant, and correctional auditor. He is also a member of the American Jail Association, American Correctional Association, Hammond Police Citizen Advisory Commission, National Sheriffs' Association, Illinois Sheriffs' Association, and former president of the Illinois Academy of Criminology. Elvis taught criminal justice at the college level and served as a fire and police commissioner.

Other Books by Elvis Slaughter

Preschool to Prison
Safer Jail and Prison Matters
The American Genocide
The Ghosts of Hollandale
Uncle Percy's Blessings
The Malcolm X Project
Epiphany Or Sin
Egomaniac
Spector

Available at Amazon.com and www.elvisslaughter.com

www.ingramcontent.com/pod-product-compliance
Lightning Source LLC
Chambersburg PA
CBHW030615290326
41930CB00049B/391